Fall of a
Nation

a Biblical perspective
of a modern problem

HERBERT M. BARBER, JR., PH.D.

WESTBOW
PRESS
A DIVISION OF THOMAS NELSON

Unless noted otherwise, all biblical references are used by permission by The Lockman Foundation (1975). New American Standard Bible.
New York: Collins Publishers.

WestBow Press books may be ordered through booksellers or by contacting:

WestBow Press
A Division of Thomas Nelson
1663 Liberty Drive
Bloomington, IN 47403
www.westbowpress.com
1-(866) 928-1240

ISBN: 978-1-4497-6573-6 (hc)
ISBN: 978-1-4497-6572-9 (sc)
ISBN: 978-1-4497-6571-2 (e)

Library of Congress Control Number: 2012916205

Printed in the United States of America

WestBow Press rev. date: 09/25/2012

For what will a man be profited if he gains
the whole world and forfeits his soul?
Matthew 16:26

Preface

America is a fallen nation. Our social structures have collapsed, our economic structures have collapsed, and the spiritual fabric of our society has collapsed.

At best, we can only hope that America is at a definitive crossroad that we will consider wisely. Do we move to the right or to the left? Do we take this path or that path? The path we chose as a nation-in-the-making for some 300 years led us to a place that could only be envied by other nations. However, along 1960 or so, America began straying from her roots, from her foundation, from what made her great. In hindsight, it is clear that America has taken the wrong path.

Yes, we were a great nation, a mighty nation, one that stood in the face of adversity as David did Goliath. With seemingly no hope, we have stood against evil, against the unrighteous, against the ungodly - right up until we too became *the ungodly*.

Prepare to pay the price of disobedience.

Introduction

America has long lived under the masquerade of capitalism, all while operating as a socialist economy. Never has this fact been more apparent than in the last few years. Of course, this became ever more apparent recently when Fannie Mae, Freddie Mac, and other mortgage companies lowered their lending requirements and local bankers knowingly loaned monies to persons with no realistic means of servicing their debt obligations. As probability would have it, not to mention a cursory review of these persons' financial statements, they quickly defaulted, leading to the immediate collapse of the entire world economy. The sheer stupidity leaves me without appropriate words of expression. While this truth runs counter to those who prefer to blame Wall Street executives for our current state of economic existence, there were no laws mandating local bankers forsake common sense and loan money to the *entitled* despite the obvious.

However, there is a larger problem that has long been brewing in America; a much larger problem, one that is destroying the very fiber of humankind itself. With no doubt, the blame for the collapse

The type of governmental structure, e.g. economic structure, countries have is a reflection of its people's obedience to God and subsequently, their attitude toward work.

1

of the US economy and subsequent world economy resulted from the poor decisions of local US bankers, but the collapse of the economy in America and elsewhere is merely symptomatic of a more sinister problem that is more damning than even socialism.

Socialism itself can trace its roots to an era long before America was a country, and while the parallels among former socialist economies are sometimes startling, the results are most often predictable. The results of socialism are not only predictable; they are consistent. Socialism most often leads to her ugly sister, communism, or some other form of dictatorship, but it nearly always leads to the downfall of economies - and life as people know it.

The Soviet Union lost the Cold War to America, politically, economically, psychologically, and literally. A socialist economy - well, a communist economy - cannot stand against a truly capitalist economy, albeit America was well on her way toward socialism at the time of the fall of the Soviet Union. Blame the eventual collapse of the Soviet Union on their war with the Afghans, Chernobyl disaster, moral decay, political corruption, or whatever; they lost the Cold War. But the ultimate collapse of their country was due in large part to socialism and communism; it eventually crushed their country.

Consider other socialist countries, e.g. Angola, China, Germany, and Vietnam. Aside from China, no socialist or communist country will result in much economically speaking; it just does not typically occur. So, why is China prospering? Eschatologically speaking, China has a significant role to play, but to play its role it must first be a formidable nation, thus the current economic boom in

China. As a side note, note that Russia is hastily working on its return as a dominate power, as Russia will also play a large role in end-time events (see Ezekiel 38-39).

For communism to exist there must first be socialism; for socialism to exist there must first be capitalism; and for capitalism to exist there must first be entrepreneurs. There must first be a society that places priority on work, or work ethic, realizing that people reap what they sow. When people sow seeds of hard work and integrity, they reap positive fruits at harvest. Conversely, when they sow seeds of slothfulness and wickedness, they reap rotten fruits at harvest.

The Bible is clear on the topic of work. The topic is discussed in multiple passages in the text. As early as Genesis 1, we find that God *worked* for six days to create the heavens and earth and concluded that His work was good. Since God is inherently good, can it not also be argued that work is also inherently good? Further, given that man is made in the image of God (see Genesis 1:27), perhaps we too are to work. Moreover, God specifically commanded us to work. "Six days you shall labor and do all your work . . ." (Exodus 20:9) Unfortunately, I am afraid these ideas come as an unwelcome surprise to an increasing number of persons in America.

Perhaps the subtle point here is that there *will* be a harvest, one way or the other. And, since we do indeed reap what we sow, is it not equally true that we control the harvest?

The type of governmental structure, e.g. economic structure, countries have is a reflection of its people's obedience to God and subsequently, their attitude toward work. Clearly there are other variables associated with the economic structure and subsequent financial success of a country, but suffice it to say, our obedience to God and our attitude toward work play a primary role in the development of this structure.

As you read through these pages, remember; *a capitalist economy allows people free reign to produce, a socialist economy controls their production, and a communist economy destroys its people.* Moreover, remember, what we choose to sow is our decision, and in a strange twist, so is our harvest.

Early Socialism

Many persons trace the roots of early socialism to Germany, a country rooted in injustice. Others trace socialism to England or France. However, the origin of socialism goes back much further. Reflect on Genesis and Exodus in the Bible a moment. These first two books in the Bible have much to say about socialism. Before we begin, it may help you to give a serious reading to these books prior to reading further in this manuscript, for if you do not have a basic understanding of Genesis and Exodus, you may be lost with the text herein, as we will begin our study with little introduction.

Let us pick up the story in Genesis. As you may recall, Egypt had recently experienced seven years of plenty, exactly as God had revealed in his dream to Joseph (see Genesis 41:29), the son of Jacob. The "land brought forth abundantly." (Genesis 41:47) The days were full of the best life had to offer, and there was plenty to go around. Both the Israelites and the Egyptians lived the good life.

Such was the case with America. Life was good. Life was not only just good; life was great! Food, clothing, and shelter; perhaps more was wasted than even consumed. Every desire was at the fingertips of the average American citizen. Over the last few decades, virtually nothing has been beyond the reach of the American citizen willing to put forth a little effort - a little work. Even uneaten food has been trucked off by the ton to landfills, all while people in other nations starve. Due to our increasing supply of waste in America, engineers have been forced to develop creative ways of dealing with our wasted surpluses, such as developing Waste to Energy facilities that transform municipal solid waste into electricity.[1]

We put a man on the moon. Why? Because we could. We created the assembly line, the computer, and all the fancy software that integrates the two. We create knowledge more rapidly than any other nation ten-fold. A hundred-fold. We are called upon to solve *every* world crisis - every famine, every manmade disaster, every natural disaster, every political skirmish, every conflict, every war. We even fight wars for other countries, and then rebuild the countries we just destroyed. America is there, and we are there with no thank you. We are wrong when we do not get involved, and we are wrong when we do get involved. Yet what is asked of us when we have given all we can possibly give? Just a little more.

We have earned huge incomes, bought expensive cars, boats, and loads of other junk we do not use and do not need. We have owned houses with rooms we rarely enter and offices packed with technology we can barely operate. For most Americans, the American Dream has become having more than you want - and substantially more than

---

[1]   Only three countries generate more waste per capita than the United States (Barber, 2011).

you need. By any measure, Americans have lived in the land of plenty.

Before we begin complimenting ourselves, however, let us quickly reflect on how America became a great nation. It can be summed up in a few words. We sought God, and he blessed. We worked, and he blessed. We obeyed, and he blessed. The more we sought God and obeyed him, the more he blessed us. The more we worked, the more he blessed. In short, we sought his will as a nation, obeyed his will as a nation, and worked toward his will as a nation - and he blessed. We obeyed; he blessed.

Such was the case for God's people in Egypt during the seven years of plenty. They sought and obeyed God, and he blessed. They worked, and he blessed. They worked more, and he blessed more - as long as they obeyed.

Recall that God revealed to his servant, Joseph, the meaning of Pharaoh's dream while he was in prison. Begin reading in Genesis 41:15.

> And Pharaoh said to Joseph, "I have had a dream, but no one can interpret it; and I have heard it said about you that when you hear a dream you can interpret it. Joseph then answered Pharaoh saying, it is not in me; God will give Pharaoh a favorable answer. So Pharaoh spoke to Joseph, "In my dream, behold, I was standing on the bank of the Nile; and behold seven cows, fat and sleek, came up out of the Nile; and they grazed in the marsh grass. And lo seven other cows came up after them, poor and very ugly and

> gaunt, such as I had never seen for ugliness in all the land of Egypt; and the lean and ugly cows ate up the first seven fat cows."

Skip verse 21 a few minutes and go to verse 22:

> I also saw in my dream, and behold, seven ears, full and good, came up on a single stalk; and lo, seven ears, withered, thin, and scorched by the east wind, sprouted up after them; and the thin ears swallowed the seven good ears . . .

In the verses that follow, Joseph interprets the dream, telling Pharaoh that the dreams are one in the same. Through Joseph, God reveals that Egypt soon will experience seven years of plenty and seven years of famine. Fortunately for Joseph and the people, Pharaoh was wise and yielded to Joseph's interpretation of the dream and in so doing, yielded to God. Due to Joseph's obedience (found earlier in the text), God appoints Joseph ruler of Egypt through Pharaoh. " . . . Since God has informed you of all this, there is no one so discerning and wise as you are. You shall be over my house . . . . I have set you over all the land of Egypt." (Genesis 41:39-41) Joseph was only 30 years old when appointed ruler of Egypt (see verse 46), a fact worth pondering, especially when we couple his age with the fact that Joseph was in prison for several years immediately prior to his appointment as ruler of Egypt.

Pharaoh then directed Joseph to prepare for the forthcoming seven years of famine that would follow the seven years of plenty. Therefore, the people worked, and

Joseph stored the grain, lest God's people perish. Let us hear that again: The people *worked*. Allow that idea to sink in a bit. *The people worked.* And as they worked, the land brought forth "abundantly." (verse 47) So "He [Joseph] gathered all the food of these seven years [during the seven years of plenty] .... and stored up grain in great abundance like the sand of the sea, until he stopped measuring it, for it was beyond measure." (Genesis 41:48-49, bracketed commentary mine)

God means this situation here for good. However, to the keenly discerning observer one sees a situation that could easily turn for the worse if not kept in check.

"When the seven years of plenty which had been in the land of Egypt came to an end, and the seven years of famine began to come, just as Joseph had said, then there was famine in all the lands; but in all the lands of Egypt there was bread (Genesis 41:53-54)." Herein lays the potential for a very serious problem. Look again at verse 30. " ... and after them [the seven years of plenty] seven years of famine will come, and all the abundance will be forgotten . . ." (bracketed commentary).

The situation in Egypt is getting more serious by the second; the people are not exactly in an envious position. The famine is ravaging the land (verse 30), and the people are starving. They now have nothing, and subsequently, they are vulnerable. Aside from the famine sweeping the land, the stage is being set for the possibility of destruction across the land.

The land in Egypt was famished - not some of the land, all of the land - and the people cried out to Pharaoh, and Pharaoh responded in verse 55 by saying, "Go to Joseph;

whatever he says to you, you shall do." Here is the sticking point: If this situation had not been ordained by God himself (see Genesis 45:8, for example), with a godly man in place for the distribution of grain, this would have proven to be a disastrous situation for the Israelites, Egyptians, and potentially the world at large from the beginning. Fortunately, God sent Joseph to *preserve* life (see Genesis 45:5).

However, the Egyptians are buying grain *from* the government here, buying what was their own grain! This situation has Socialism 101 written all over it. History has clearly demonstrated that on its best day, government is synonymous with power, control, corruption, and ultimately, destruction.

In Genesis 47, God's people now find themselves completely broke; they have no money for they have spent it merely to survive. Give some thought to where America is now. Are you beginning to draw the parallels and see the potential for power, corruption, control, and destruction (and in that order)? As for now, God sees this situation in the text necessary for the preservation of his people, but the possibility for godless power, control, corruption, and destruction remains alive and well.

...the Egyptians are buying grain from the government here, buying what was their own grain! This situation has Socialism 101 written all over it.

"And when the money was all spent in the land of Egypt and in the land of Canaan, all the Egyptians came to Joseph and said, 'Give us food, for why should we die in your presence? (verse 15).'" This is classic socialism.

"Give me." We can take this demand at least two ways. One, the land and the fruits thereof should be those of the people, not the government, which in turn means that all land and its fruits belong to the people in the first place, not to the government so it can do as it sees fit. Somewhat conversely, perhaps the people are demanding something for which they feel they are entitled, with no compensation due thereto, though some perhaps have not worked and prepared for the seven years of famine.

Were the people entitled as those who recently purchased homes in the United States with no means to service their debt were? Were they entitled even if their entitlement had the potential to destroy the entire world economy?

Where does America currently stand economically? For that matter, where does our world stand currently? As men say when their vehicle has problems, "It's tore up." Or, as women often say, "It's broke! It needs fixin!" Our economy is broken! And worse, our country is broke, figuratively and literally.

The collective total of having our social and economic systems simultaneously in disarray is beyond our ability to correct. We are fighting a losing battle. Oh, we may win this battle or that battle, but overall, we are losing the war. Only God can repair what we have destroyed, and unfortunately God will not intervene on behalf of an ungodly people who are unwilling to humble themselves to their own Creator (see 2 Chronicles 7:14) and work. Consequently, it *will* get worse in America, and the world, much worse . . .

> Then Joseph said, "Give up your livestock, and I will give you food for your livestock, since your money is gone" [Would you not think the people would have seen a red flag go up here?]. So they brought their livestock

11

> to Joseph, and Joseph gave them food in
> exchange for the horses and the flocks and
> the herds and the donkeys; and he fed them
> with food in exchange for all their livestock
> that year (Genesis 47:16-17, bracketed
> commentary mine).

Consider the painful reality of this situation. The people have given away their horses, flocks, herds, and donkeys in exchange for food. Talk about a barter system! We give you everything we have left, and we get only a little food in return? I guess desperate times call for desperate measures.

What were God's people thinking? This situation in and of itself is riddled with huge red flags. How do they plan to overcome such a horrific yet seemingly necessary decision? How do we as Americans plan to overcome such horrific decisions we have made in the past regarding our economic situation and socio-political climate? Fortunately for God's people in Egypt, Joseph is a God-fearing man, but America's so-called leaders are not God-fearing people. Quite the contrary. Using "American leaders" and "God-fearing" in the same sentence makes for quite the oxymoron. Almost as bad, many Americans are simply lazy. They are sorry. Too sorry to work but not too sorry to take, for they will take whatever we allow.

For what good is it to give the entitled everything for which we work so hard? (At least in the biblical account, the people had initially worked.) Where does constantly giving handouts to the sorry, the entitled, leave us? Look at Genesis 41:21 that we skipped earlier; here we find that even after the seven ugly cows devoured the seven fat and sleek cows, they were "just as ugly as before." They were *still* ugly. Nothing changed.

The *entitled* have eaten away every ounce of bounty we working Americans have ever considered earning, and they are *still ugly.* We have given them free educations, free meals, free housing, free medical, free cell phones, handout after handout, subsidy after subsidy, and they're *still ugly!* You cannot change sorry. It is like paddling a boat with no bottom. You are going down; it is just a matter of time.

Nonetheless, God's people ate for another year. But note how they ate. They ate at the mercy of the government and, worse, they ate at the sacrifice of all of their tools that were necessary to support their future existence. As if that is not bad enough, the situation is about to get even worse. Consider the next few verses . . .

The Israelites are completely at the mercy of the government. Completely. Moreover friend, so are we.

> And when that year was ended, they came to him the next year and said to him [Joseph], "We will not hide from my lord that our money is all spent, and the cattle are my lord's. There is nothing left for my lord except our bodies and our hands. Why should we die before your eyes, both we and our land? Buy us and our land. Buy us [Yes, you read that correctly - *Buy us!*] and our land for food, and we and our land will be slaves [Yes, SLAVES!] to Pharaoh . . . So they said, "You have saved our lives! [Oh my! This has end day prophecy written all over it!] Let us find favor in the sight of my lord, and we

will be Pharaoh's slaves." (Genesis 47:18-19
& 25, bracketed commentary mine)

Talk about jumping out of the grease and into the fire!
Should Joseph be consumed by the power bestowed him, the
situation will quickly move through the process of control,
corruption, and destruction. The people have now given
up everything, and worse, they essentially have no way
to fend for themselves. Are we as Americans not heading
quickly down this same path? Or, are we already there? The
Israelites are completely at the mercy of the government.
Completely. Moreover friend, so are we.

America is in a nearly identical place, outside of one
significant fact. Our leaders are certainly no Joseph,
especially Obama. From the looks of things, neither will our
next president be. The current Republican front-runner,
Mitt Romney, is not a Christian either, rather a Mormon.
Of course, unlike our current president, Romney is not
anti-American. And unlike our current president, Romney
did hold a real job prior to seeking office. One of the earlier
2012 front-runners, Rick Perry, is a Christian, but he has
never as much as run a lemonade stand. He has never created
a single job. He has never met a single payroll. He is, after
all, a life-long politician. Where have the true God-fearing
leaders gone?

The only similarity between Obama and Joseph is perhaps
arrogance, but even then, Joseph's early tendency toward
arrogance was tempered years before he was 30, i.e. before
he was appointed ruler of Egypt. I guess the "pit" has a
way of dealing with arrogance - especially when you throw
slavery and imprisonment in on top of it. Obama is in his
early 50s, and his arrogance reigns supreme. Unfortunately,

his arrogance could not run more counter to his actual (positive) accomplishments as the leader of the free world! Even worse, given that the Republican Party seems to be having difficulty getting its own party in order, Obama may actually have a chance to rule another four years, thus, sealing the catastrophic fate of America once and for all.

Consider our modern day economy. Obama did more to destroy America in his first two years in office than the collective damage reaped from all politicians since the founding of this country. Many of his own people do not even want him in office anymore. However, Obama knows *exactly* what he is doing. He is no fool; he just hates America. He is logarithmically more anti-American than any ten thousand terrorists. He has inflicted more damage on the American economy than all natural disasters to hit our soils combined - and then some. The American Dream is over.

It appears that the Israelites are not the only people who have jumped out of the grease and into the fire. Any dreams of success God's people had are now resting entirely upon the provisions managed by a single man, at best. However, remember, up until this point in the story, the Israelites are being led by a man ordained of God. We, my friend, are not led by a man ordained of God. We are led by a man engulfed with Satan, himself.

You may have heard it said that of the 56 men who signed the Declaration of Independence, approximately 54 were Christians. Only God knew their hearts, but assuming that is true, we have come a long way as a nation. Today we probably could not find 54 born-again Christians in all of Congress.

Consider what happens to economies when they are not led by Godly men and women. Flip to the book of Exodus. Picking up the text in verse six of the first chapter, we find that Joseph has died, as well as his brothers and the balance of that generation. Not to belabor the point, but this is a crucial point in history. Joseph and the generations before him was a God-fearing people, and now an entire generation has died and with it all that embodied that generation, as we will see. This sounds strikingly analogous to America.

Let us consider where we are as a nation, as a people. For example, my great grandfather came to America in 1654 from Yorkshire, England. He was one of the first British to arrive on American soil after colonization began. Dr. Luke Barber, a surgeon in the Cromwell Court of England, no doubt weathered many storms crossing the raging Atlantic seas on the *Golden Fortune* just to get to America. He came in the name of freedom from a corrupt government and the freedom to worship. He eventually owned 1,200 acres of land and became one of the early governors of Maryland. He came for the same reasons as most others at the time, a full 122 long years before the United States was even founded. (Yet corrupt government officials who are a mere one generation removed from their countries elsewhere, tell *us* what we can and cannot do?)

Dr. Barber's family settled large areas of Maryland, North Carolina, South Carolina, Georgia, and Florida. One of his great grandsons and my great grandfather, Obadiah Barber, was one of the most prominent people of his time to live in the southeastern United States. Today he is well known for his association with the Land of the Trembling Earth, the Okefenokee Swamp, and Obadiah's Okefenok.

Picture the scene; we have this large influx of people coming to America, all traveling here for the same reasons, for the most part. Yet over the course of several generations since ole Grandpa Luke moved to America, something changed, something that would have devastating repercussions upon America. We forgot the very reason we founded America - freedom *from* government and freedom *from* religious persecution (or rather, *prosecution*). We sought God, we obeyed God, and we labored according to his will.

Arguably, we established what would become the greatest nation humankind has known. Unfortunately, with the passing of time, America would abandon her ties with God and her work ethic, and self-destruct under the weight of what would become a sick nation ran by a godless people - exactly as we saw with God's people in Genesis and Exodus.

Practical Socialism in America

Socialism comes in many forms. In its most fundamental form, the act of socialism occurs anytime someone takes something that he has not earned from someone who has. It is very similar to, if not in fact, stealing. It is legalized stealing, and persons who complete these acts cross all socioeconomic boundaries and cultures in America. White, black, and purple. Christians, Catholics, Mormons, and tree huggers. It does not matter. Socialism pulls no punches. Its sole objective is to destroy economies, and it offers no apologies for doing so.

One of the earliest forms of socialism in America began when Abraham Lincoln implemented a biased tax structure through which unequal taxes would be paid based upon work ethic and subsequent earnings. How foolish. The more you worked, the more taxes you paid. The smarter you were, the more taxes you paid. The more successful you were, the more taxes you paid. Of course, the reciprocal was equally as true. The less you worked, the fewer taxes you paid.

Congress created the tax structure for the purposes of paying war expenses. Too bad whether you were in favor of the Civil War or against it; that was irrelevant. Congress, i.e. the government, thought you should pay. By the way, have you ever wondered whether those imposed taxes paid for the war expenses of both the North and the South, or just the expenses of the North?

The tax structure had socialism written all over it from the beginning. When the 16th Amendment was enacted several years later, Congress levied a one percent tax on net personal incomes over $3,000 and six percent on personal incomes over $500,000. (IRS, 2011) This represents one of the earliest acts toward socialism in the United States.

Closely consider the first tax mandate. Persons had to pay a one percent tax on net personal incomes over $3,000. What about those persons who made $2,999? They paid nothing! What about those persons who made $10,000 or $100,000? What about persons who made over half a million? They paid more - much, much more! What about the sorry people? What about the people who were too sorry to work? They all reaped the same exact benefits from the government. They all drove on the same roads, such as they were; and they all received the same military protection, such as it was. Just like today. We pay *unequal* taxes, yet we all receive equal benefits (well, not exactly; takers always take more than they contribute). Why would we remotely consider this biased tax structure fair? There is nothing fair about it. It amounts to stealing from those who *choose* to work hard.

As America's history has proven, it is impossible to successfully integrate persons having an average IQ of 85 with persons having an average IQ of 102.

Put this in modern day terms. Why should I have to pay more in taxes than you pay? You drive on the same road on which I drive. When we both purchase candy bars at the convenience store, they do not charge you one price and me another, do they? Of course not. When we both purchase a car from the local car dealer, do they charge you more because you are rich and I am poor? No. Is your arm broken? Are you just lazy? Or, are you just sorry? Then why would we not have a flat tax in this country for every adult? We all pay the same exact amount (not percentage) of money to cover our taxes, and nothing more.

Everyone wants a fair tax structure; right up until it is actually fair. Half of the people in this country pay no federal income taxes, period! How is this fair? More people than that do not pay taxes, actually, if you count government workers. Yet all these people drive on the same roads. They live in houses that are not theirs. They eat food that is not theirs, and their kids eat school lunches that are not theirs. While their kid's free lunch was free to them, I can assure you that their kid's free lunch was not free for me. Neither were their medical bills.

Some will argue that a flat tax should be based upon a percentage, implying that the more you earn, the more you use government resources, infrastructure, and the like. While this opinion is not completely correct, most private sector taxpayers would prefer this method to most of the people in this country paying no taxes period.

Of course, when our socialized tax system was implemented, we needed people to enforce it. Enter the Internal Revenue System (IRS). The IRS also traces its roots to Lincoln. It is also worth noting that Lincoln fought to pass the Emancipation Proclamation in an attempt to abolish slavery, and while slavery should have never occurred in this country, neither should have the importation of slaves.

Importation and integration has done nothing more than dumb down America, literally.

As America's history has proven, it is impossible to successfully integrate persons having an average IQ of 85 with persons having an average IQ of 102. Given a standard deviation of 10, persons with an IQ of 85 score nearly two standard deviations lower than persons with an IQ of 102 - a huge difference, statistically. This issue becomes even more serious when attempting to integrate both of these groups with persons having IQs of, say 110-130+. This intelligence issue is of monumental importance in the United States, but it is downplayed and ignored as if this issue does not exist. Statistically speaking and practically speaking, this is hugely significant! This is not racism; rather, it is a matter of race. It is a simple matter of fact, and there is an extensive body of research to substantiate these facts.

Looking again at the IRS, laws associated with the tax structure in the US are so complicated that the IRS employs over 100,000 persons, and these 100,000 persons use their $13-14 billion budget (IRS, 2011) gladly to serve essentially as cops over "We the People."

Have you ever dealt with an IRS employee? They have no names; they have no faces. Notice how they correspond with you . . . through a damning *anonymous* letter. They stand behind the shield of the federal government, and they can do no wrong. They charge you penalties for filing late, yet refuse to render you interest for holding onto overpayments or the like on your part for months and even years. Worse, in some states the IRS and/or states deliberately delay reimbursement of your money. If they think you owe them money, they take your money directly from your financial accounts and ask questions later. After you spend years convincing them that their rampage on your financial accounts was unwarranted due to their error, it takes months and years before they return your money. Again, forget about them paying you interest on the money they stole from you; you will never get it. Why do they do this? Because we let them. They stand behind the shield of the federal government, behind their counters, behind their glass walls, and say, "I can do no wrong; I am the government; I am powerful. I am all-powerful - and you are nothing but a lowly taxpayer (a slave). I make the rules, and you abide by the rules I make."

I once called the IRS to check on a rather large sum they owed me. After stumbling through the endless recordings and selections, I was automatically placed on hold - 47 minutes to be exact. Then I talked with one of their brightest tax scholars. Then I talked with another tax scholar. Then I talked with yet another tax scholar. I was told they had no record of my having ever filed for this sum at all, even with me holding the claim in my hands and having signed receipts of its delivery and acceptance. However, do not worry; they certainly have never had a problem finding all of the money I have paid them over the years.

Consider another encounter I had with the IRS. As a business owner, I often wait until October to pay the previous year's taxes, like many business owners. It is a smart strategy for businesses as they can then leverage their tax monies as capital for other endeavors for the first nine or ten months of the year. Doing so, the savvy professional can turn that sum into an even larger sum, and then pay their taxes in October along with a relatively small penalty.

This idea is not unique with me; it is common. Once when holding back to pay my taxes until October, an IRS agent barged into my office demanding *her* money. I wasn't even late! It was a sizable amount of money, and they wanted their cut - and they wanted it now! She boldly stated that *she* would withdraw funds from my accounts if I refused to pay immediately or worse, put me in jail. This is what happens when we abandon God and allow the ungodly in our society to rule.

The fact is, the less you earn in this country, the more subsidized you are, the more freebies government employees force the rest of us pay. The more you want, the more I must work; and the more I work, the more you want. The more you sit on your porch, the more I must work. Do you really think I like getting up at three o'clock in the morning to catch a 6:00am flight to earn money so you can steal 75 or 80 percent of my money because you are too lazy to try? Do you think I like staying away from my family night after night working while you receive a lifetime membership at the food stamp office? Do you think I like pulling up to a Waffle House at one o'clock in the morning to eat dinner after late meetings, only to then have to get up at three to catch a flight to the next city, all so you can live in free housing for life, or for that matter, while you teach school 180 days out of the year and complain the other 185 days about how tough you have it because your summer, spring, fall, and Christmas vacations are too short? Do you think I like paying thousands and thousands in taxes so you can teach one class a semester in your job as a college professor and your wife refines her brownie-making skills as a stay-at-home mom rather than helping to pay for the roads on which she drives? Do you think I enjoy watching one government employee dig a hole while five others watch? Or, do you think I like to watch my business struggle over and over in this economy while you take out farm subsidies? Do you think I want to struggle with all my might to earn some meager form of retirement while you swagger in and out of your government job 30 years and then expect the rest of us to pay for your retirement for the next 40 years? Or worse, you barely work and then live off of government handouts?

The truth hurts. *The more I give, the more you want!* That is practical socialism in America, by definition. Apparently, this is the sole reason we have the IRS - to take money from those who do and give it to those who do not. I have concluded that this is the sole reason we have government in this country. This is what happens when a society - its people and its leaders - abandon God.

Are you certain you want to chase the American Dream? Really? You want to earn a strong education and work like a dog to have a strong income, to make something out of your life? Be prepared to pay a price, for it will cost you deeply to succeed in this country. You will soon learn that success in America is laced with many dark, lonely failures, failures that are only worsened when you realize that you are carrying significantly more than your fair share of the tax burden. Nonetheless, welcome to America.

God's word tells us that we reap what we sow (see Gal. 6:7) and more than we sow

For the last 40 or 50 years, America has increasingly sown bad seeds. Very bad seeds. Now we are reaping the harvest from those bad seeds – the utter destruction of the very spiritual, moral, social, and economic fabric upon which this country was founded.

(see Matthew 13:23), and we know that we reap later than we sow. Of course, this should be no problem for those who have sown good seeds, seeds of righteousness. However, it is a very serious matter for those who have sown bad seeds, or for those who suffer due to others sowing bad seeds.

For the last 40 or 50 years, America has increasingly sown bad seeds, very bad seeds. Now we are reaping the harvest from those bad seeds - the destruction of the very spiritual, moral, social, and economic fabric upon which this country was founded. We have sown bad seeds for so long in America that we have begun to believe our selection of seeds to be the best that can be sown. Why would we believe anything else? We are the United States of America, the greatest country to ever exist.

Oh how wrong we are. Our success as a nation has dissolved our dependency on God - and there is a price to be paid.

Consider a few basic examples of practical socialism in our lives. We see these examples play out every day, but we have become desensitized to them, so much so that taking from those who do and giving to those who do not is now a way of life in America - the rule rather than the exception. In reality, it is nothing more than stealing.

Public schools here mandate that kids have a breakfast and lunch account. Parents pay into that account weekly or monthly and kids draw against that account to eat. At the high school level kids are allowed to purchase whatever they want and how much they want on any given day. Last school year my high school son's account accidentally ran down to zero; he had no money in his account, so they refused to let him eat. Sorry, son; you have no money in your account. No money; no food. Therefore, my son went hungry that day. If this were the end of the story, I would have no problem, but the story does not end here. What about the countless kids in line behind my son whose lunches were free? They pay nothing for lunch - every day of the year. They pay nothing for breakfast - every day of the year. Five days a week, they eat free meals, all at my expense . . . . because their parents are lifetime members of the US Welfare Club.

This scene plays out every day in America. Because I have worked my fingers to the bones for years earning a good education, and because I *choose* every day to work rather than sit on the front porch, my son goes hungry while a kid with lazy parents takes food from my son's mouth? Your kid's nourishment is not my problem, or any taxpayer's, especially when you are too lazy to help provide for him. If he goes hungry, so be it. The few people left who actually work and pay taxes can only support so many free lunches, contrary to the "be all you can be at other people's expense" movement in this country. By the way, we now feed these same kids on Saturdays, as well. Of course, the good news is that you do have to qualify first - if your parents work for a living, for example, you don't qualify. Sorry.

While we are on the subject of food, consider this example. A school teacher who attends our church felt God leading her to start a program she called "Backpack Buddies." The program was considered a worthwhile endeavor. We attend a rather large church, so there was no shortage of persons willing to help. The idea was to have people bring a food good or two to church every Wednesday night, package them, and distribute them to needy school children the following day so their families could have food to eat. Well, as the story goes, everyone brought food goods the first Wednesday night, and they anxiously packed the recently purchased backpacks full of food - a ton of them. Designated persons then delivered the new backpacks filled with free food to the kids at school the following morning. So far so good. However, that was the first and last time they were able to use the backpacks. Rather than returning the backpacks to school the next day as they were instructed, they stole the backpacks! They stole them! They were never returned, even after being asked to return them. Talk about biting the hand that feeds you! You cannot change sorry. You might as well argue against ignorance. You lose - every time.

We could go on and on with stories like these, giving example after example of practical socialism. What about people who live off food stamps their entire lives? You know these people - the people you wait behind in the grocery store while they unload five gallons of free milk for the week while talking on their government cell phone and getting out their government debit card.

How many times have you ridden by the housing projects in your city only to see hundreds of people sitting idly by on the front porch? Already seen and done it all in life; just waiting to die. Really? Are you telling me that these strapping twenty and thirty year olds can't work? Or the 40, 50, and 60 year olds, for that matter? This situation is so bad in my town that they no longer sit on the porches; they are usually having a big barbeque or chili cook-off on a vacant lot.

They make a definitive decision every single day to live like this, yet over half of America feel sorry for them (Usually the half that aren't paying for them to eat!). "Poor Leroy.

He's only 25; he looks so tired, so helpless. How sad. I bet his back is hurting him today. He must have twisted it playing basketball down at the court yesterday. Poor thing. You know, it is a good thing Leroy had his government subsidized cell phone with him when he twisted his back yesterday. Otherwise, he may have laid there for hours waiting on the ambulance to get there." Practical socialism.

Have you ever been to the emergency room on a Saturday for something relatively minor, like what appears to be a bad cold, sprained ankle, or cut that needs a couple of stitches? Sorry, sir. I know you are a paying patient, but you will have to wait until we first help Shaweekwa - despite the fact that she is not paying. Practical socialism.

My wife tells the story that one day her friend was sitting in the waiting room to see her physician. After sitting a while and seeing many people go in ahead of her, she finally went to the counter and loudly exclaimed, "Hey, why don't you help your paying patients first, rather than catering to all these non-paying people?" Practical socialism.

How about higher education? How many quotas has there been over the years for so-called minorities? This is blatant discrimination. People are accepted into schools all over this country based on the color of their skin, not academic history or academic promise. How pathetic; and *For those learned in measurement and statistics, integration is viewed as nothing more than another failed social experiment by do-gooders.* they are not much better off when they finish, if they do, than they were before they started because they are floated through the system. Yet, many in America think this is fair. Many Americans not only think this is fair, they think this is *right*. After all, it is the American way. Take from those who *do* and give to those who do not.

These people are given something they did not earn and did not deserve. For example, when I applied for admissions for my first earned doctorate, I was asked to retake a standardized entrance exam. They wanted my scores to be a little higher. Therefore, I retook the exam, my scores improved, and I was accepted. However, this is not the end to the story, not by far. During my first semester in the program when I was talking to one of the employees who handled admissions for the doctoral program my eyes were opened. She said, "Too bad you aren't black. Your first scores were easily high enough to be admitted." So what were my grades in degrees prior to applying and then having to take the standardized exam again? Straight A's. This is how practical socialism plays out in our daily lives.

Before we leave our educational system, consider integration. Some people felt it would be wise to integrate our schools some years ago. That sounds noble until you consider the substantially different levels of intelligence among races and the affect such would have on the races in general, not to mention, our educational system. Well, we are now reaping what happens when you try to integrate students with an average IQ of 102 with those who have an average IQ of 85. For those of you who understand measurement and statistics, you immediately realize that this is a huge problem. It is a mathematical impossibility to reap anything positive from such a decision. As previously stated, that is a difference of nearly two whole standard deviations. For those learned in measurement and statistics, integration is viewed as nothing more than another failed social experiment by do-gooders.

However, that being said, I am not suggesting that one race is better than another race. All men and women are created in the image of God (Genesis 1:27), and we all have our strengths and weaknesses, but remember; God separated the races for a reason, whatever that was. It is simply a fact that many refuse to accept.

On average, whites score nearly two full standard deviations higher than blacks on intelligence testing, and Asians score slightly higher than whites. Does this mean that Asians should support whites? Or that whites should support blacks? Of course not.

Consider another example. Black athletes nearly always outperform white athletes in athletic events. This fact is no more surrounded by racial overtones than these statements regarding intelligence; it is a reality, and we have to accept it.

Any disagreement with these facts does not negate their reality. Integration has proven to be as bad as inter-marriage; it dumbs down America. Perhaps God separated us for a reason. Even given the baseless argument sometimes made that intelligence is not derived from hereditary, if we allow for a mere one percent of intelligence to be attributable to heredity, that mandates that we are dumbing down one of the races in an inter-racial marriage and in so doing, dumbing down America.

Data always regress toward the mean, and while the constructs associated with IQ are far more complex than this book allows, even commonsense tells us that children are products of their parents (heredity) and their environment.

Children from a white parent with an IQ of 102 and a black parent with an IQ of 85 will most often yield children with IQs that are lower than children who are born to parents with IQs around 102. Of course, we do not expect a child's IQ to be the exact average of that of its parents, but you get my point.

Such is the case in an educational setting. It is impossible to simultaneously teach a student with lower intelligence with a student of average intelligence or superior intelligence. It mandates that teachers teach at the lower level and a slower pace. Schools and universities are forced to teach toward the lowest common denominator, yet we blame teachers and professors when American students fall behind other nations academically. Nonetheless, we have integration because a few do-gooders thought it was the right thing to do, and we have a weaker America to show for it. Practical socialism.

What about farmers? They are part of the backbone of America, and several of my friends come from farming families, but farmers receive government-backed loans every day. Farming is a business, just like other businesses. When times are good, they profit, and when times are bad, they struggle. Such is not the case when it comes to farming, however. Through private sector taxpayers, the government backs farming loans; this typically does not occur when it comes to other businesses. Even worse, the government pays many farmers not to farm - not to work - apparently to keep competition in check. Unfortunately, those who participate in such schemes further destroy America; they take what is not theirs to take. Practical socialism.

When my wife was earning her MBA, she met a young woman who told her that she was applying for a grant so she too could buy a house. Most people would never be aware of such a handout. This woman grew up this way - taking from the system while contributing little to nothing in return. She was soon to have an MBA, one of the world's most envied academic degrees, yet she was looking for a handout. Practical socialism.

Consider what we refer to as modern day welfare. Franklin Roosevelt is credited for establishing the Social Security System in the US, establishing the program back in the 1930s. By any standard, it has been an utter failure. For example, after the course of a 30-year career that averaged, say, $35,000 a year, you personally contributed $80,000 at best toward Social Security. However, this is not all you draw. You also draw from contributions made by your employer, a form of forced socialism; and you draw from what other people have contributed. And, we all just close our eyes, hold hands, and assume that somehow all will be well.[2]

During one of the early GOP debates for the 2012 presidential election, Rick Perry gave us a perfect example of how he encouraged practical socialism in the state of Texas. He essentially said this: He is for border protection, but if people do get in, their children will receive a free college education. Huh? Perhaps his years as a government worker have over shadowed his formative years of working with his parents on their farm. He seems to have no idea how he receives his government paycheck. It just shows

---

[2] The average monthly draw from Social Security is currently $1,177 a month, or $272 a week (Internal Revenue Service, 2011).

up every month. Perry claims giving these people a free education helps them not become a drain on the system. Huh? If they are in our country illegally, they already are draining a system to which they have not contributed. Send them packing!

Perry's comments bring to mind a woman's comments she posted on Facebook during that same debate. She said, "Hey, I pay taxes. Where is my handout?" Ironic she would be of this opinion given that she is a public school teacher who only pays taxes off the taxes of private sector taxpayers.

A few years ago, the government gave the auto industry several billion dollars to bail them out of financial collapse. It just needed a little boost, you might say - just a few billion should do the trick. For years, Administration after Administration has discussed the financial woes associated with the US automotive industry, especially those with ties to Detroit. The current Administration is no different. We hear about Detroit often - and rightly so. There are major issues that need addressing, albeit not by the federal government.

The auto industry is arguably a large part of the backbone of the American economy. In total, it employs 1.71 million people in the US and makes up 2.7 percent of the gross domestic product (US Department of Commerce, 2011). It has well established unions and lobbyists, and the current Administration has gone to great lengths to prop up the failing industry by giving them billions upon billions of dollars with no strings attached.

Is it good fiscal policy to prop up an industry in a capitalist country, and if so, who is to say which industries are propped up? Those who have never created a job or met a payroll?

For example, contrast the US automotive industry with the US construction industry. While the US automotive industry employees 1.71 million people, the US construction industry employed roughly 8.1 million people in 2007 before the economic collapse (US Department of Commerce, 2011), including construction employees listed only in the construction sector. It made up 4.83 percent of the US gross domestic product, nearly twice that of the auto industry, and employed nearly three times as many employees. Yet it has been completely overlooked by virtually all administrations - forever.

Politicians and economists use home construction as a method of gauging economic prosperity, while disregarding infrastructure construction, heavy civil construction, commercial construction, and most importantly, industrial construction. Since 2007-08, there has essentially been no construction activity in the US and relatively little throughout the world. Yet, despite evidence that would strongly support propping up the construction industry over the auto industry, Congress chose to prop up an industry that clearly contributes significantly less to our gross domestic product - our economic well-being.

If we lived in a truly capitalistic economy, the government would not prop up any industry - because the government would never have the resources to do so in the first place. When a government has the financial means to bailout *any* industry, that government is too big. Companies within the auto

When a government has the financial means to bailout any industry, that government is too big.

industry or construction industry would simply fail, and in turn, their customer base would be absorbed by other companies, or the industry itself would dissolve.

Of course, Obama supposedly wanted to prop up the construction industry with infrastructure projects. Unfortunately, this will not work. This is not a solid temporary fix, let alone a permanent fix. For the construction industry to be propped up, projects would have to be those that created sustainable jobs, meaning that the government would only fund projects that would be constructed and then have private sector businesses operating in these built structures - immediately stimulating the economy. Simply building a bridge usually does not stimulate the economy for long, in and of itself, as there is no potential for long-term economic growth (unless that particular bridge serves as a catalyst for substantial economic development in a region, which is usually unlikely). There must always be private sector jobs associated with the project after it is constructed, in some form, for this method of stimulating the economy to work. Otherwise, our country simply incurs more debt we cannot pay.

Briefly consider Obama's attempt to further socialize America through his jobs law. It is a great example of how to destroy an economy. His ideas all center on hiring more government employees, and he has done just that. He wants to take even more of our hard-earned money and hire more teachers, firemen, policemen, and social workers - or at least keep the ones we have. This is a foolish attempt to keep an economy going; it never has, it doesn't, and it won't. When is the last time a fireman created a job? Never. Government employees do not create jobs.

Certainly, some government positions are indeed necessary, and some government employees are great at their jobs. They are fantastic people, but nonetheless, there is a surplus of government employees, and this surplus is unsustainable.

When is the last time the lunchroom person at your kid's school created a job? How about employees with the Department of Transportation? The Department of Agriculture or the Environmental Protection Agency? How about the electrician at the local community college or the dean? These people are wonderful, but they are just like all government employees. They take from those who make. Any contributions from nearly all government employees toward stimulating the economy come from monies that were already in the economy via private taxpayers. Thus, their economic contribution is non-existent in terms of positively stimulating the economy.

Further, any monies they receive in the form of income are likely to be detrimental to the economy as they take money from those persons who truly do stimulate the economy. Nonetheless, we regularly praise these people for their valiant efforts, for their hard work. The next time you see a government employee being hailed as a hero, thank a private sector taxpayer who works 70 hours a week taking enormous financial risks to make their heroism possible.

Certainly, many government employees do care about the service they provide the rest of us. Many are strong Christians - and will receive many crowns in Heaven. However, we not only do not need many of the services provided by these employees, we cannot afford them. When the average private sector employee annually earns $50,462, plus $10,589 in benefits (Cauchon, 2010), and the average federal employee receives $81,258, plus $41,791 in benefits (Cauchon, 2010), plus retirement income for life, there is something wrong. Government workers make substantially more than those who put food in their mouths!

Look on a larger scale as to how practical socialism plays out in America. Let us return to the tax system, and review what each state pays the federal government each year. Of the 50 states, 31 states take more from the federal government than they contribute (Tax Foundation, 2011). How is this fair? Why do we expect the people in one state to pay for another state's problems?

New Mexico receives $2.03 for every dollar they pay to the federal government. That's more than twice what they contribute! Why is New Mexico my problem or your problem? Most people do not know a single person who lives in New Mexico, but talk about a return on investment! They receive more than twice what they contribute year after year. Who wouldn't take this type of investment? Of course, herein is the problem. It is not an investment at all; it is stealing. You can couch it or cover it up any way you want, but at the end of the day, it is stealing, and nothing more.

Mississippi is next on the list. Mississippians take $2.02 for every dollar they contribute. Then there is Alaska, and of course, Louisiana, the state that expected the rest of us to bail them out because they were not bright enough to construct their city on the Gulf of Mexico above sea level - or at least leave when the storm was approaching. The returns for these states are 1.84 and 1.78, respectively. Nice returns, you might say. Apparently, they are indeed smarter than the rest of us. They pay no federal income taxes, yet their vote counts as much as each private sector taxpayer's vote. Explain how this borders on being anything but socialism.

The right to vote in this country should be a derivative of whether one pays taxes in this country - and how much. Merely taking up space in this country should not entitle one to vote.

What about the states on the other end of the scale, the states that financially support the 62 percent of the states who bleed them dry? Topping this list is New Jersey. The taxpayers of New Jersey receive a paltry 61 cents of every dollar they pay the federal government. Then there is Nevada and Connecticut, which only receive 65 cents and 69 cents, respectively, of every dollar they pay. Why should these states be expected to give away their hard-earned money to states their residents have never even visited? Why would they? What is even worse is the fact that these taker-states think they are entitled to take what is not theirs to take. For example, Gulf Coast Louisianans became upset when they felt the federal government did not rescue them quickly enough after Katrina (though it was later proven to be the fault of their own governor and mayor) - despite the fact that their state actually contributes absolutely nothing to the federal government. Nothing!

These numbers speak volumes regarding socialism. This line of thinking is seriously flawed, but it is a wonderful example of how the United States has been destroyed as a nation.

Consider the percentage of persons who filed a tax return in 2009 but reported no income or tax liability. This percentage was a whopping 41.7 percent (Tax Foundation, 2011), an unbelievable percentage. Worse, that number was estimated to be 46.4 percent in 2011 (Eicheler, 2011). Also, note that these percentages are taken from persons who actually bothered to file returns. Millions of people do not file altogether. To make it worse, remember that of those who did file a return and pay their taxes, a portion of these included government filers, persons who only pay taxes off the monies of private sector taxpayers.

However, this was in 2009, two to three years after the local bankers on Main Street destroyed our nation's economy and the economy of nearly every single country. Numerous people no longer have strong incomes and the subsequent tax liabilities to accommodate them. Consider years 2005 and 2006. In 2005 and 2006, 32.6 percent and 33 percent of filers paid no taxes. Look at 2007 and afterwards; and again, percentages are only for those persons who actually filed returns - and this counts government employees.

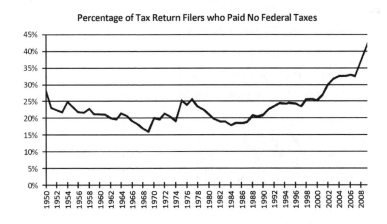

Percentage of Tax Return Filers who Paid No Federal Taxes

Data Source: (Tax Foundation, 2011)

Consider what has occurred since 1950, overall. From, say 1953 through 1983, the percentage of tax filers who paid no federal taxes remained somewhat flat, say plus or minus two percentage points (SD=2.268). However, since 1984 that percentage has increased from 18 percent in 1984 to 42 percent in 2007; and as noted earlier, to 46 percent in 2011. Since the US economy collapsed in 2007, that percentage has increased from 33 percent to 46 percent, a 40 percent increase. Unfortunately, in reality we know that these percentages are much higher than that noted, as a large portion of the population does not file tax returns at all - in addition to the fact that many of those who do file are government employees.[3]

We consistently have a large percentage of people in this country year after year, decade after decade, who choose to take what is not theirs to take, e.g. driving on roads of which they have not paid, placing their kids in public schools, or utilizing taxpayer housing. Since the early 1980s, that number has increased drastically, and it is currently skyrocketing out of control.

Where would America be if these people worked in the private sector and contributed to the economy rather than stealing from the rest of us? Where would America be if we all sat around and did nothing? It is surprising that we have been able to hang on this long as a nation. However, this luxury is quickly ending. When we model those data, we estimate that a full 100 percent of all tax filers will pay no federal income tax roughly 43 years from today if allowed to continue. Who will then pay for these persons'

---

[3]   Seventeen percent (17%) of those persons who work in the US are employed by the local, state, or federal governments (Gallup Economy, 2010). However, this percentage has greatly risen since this article was written due to Obama's hiring frenzy of government workers. In addition, several states' percentage of government workers is well above the national average of 17 percent. Alaska, Virginia, and Maryland, for example, have government workforces of 31 percent, 27 percent, and 26 percent, respectively – huge drains on the US economy.

food, clothing, and shelter - and cell phones and educations, and . . . ?

People are exploding with anger over this economic situation, and rightly so. Consider the protests that occurred week after week in the state of Ohio recently. Boy were they upset; they hung out for weeks inside their state capitol. However, it is not important why they were there as much as it is to know who these people were. They were government employees, most who are used to receiving what they have not have earned on their own merits; but why were they upset? Well, frankly, private taxpayers could no longer financially support the ever-increasing number of free loaders, and though their governor made an admirable attempt to cut them off, the takers eventually did what they always do; they took. Suffice it to say, it is not those who take who should be angry; it is those who *make* who should be angry.

Again, this is not to say that government employees are bad people, not by any means. That is far from the point here. Some are strong Christians who are employed by various government entities. However, we have created a system in the US where private sector citizens are literally controlled by the government, and controlled by the government means being controlled by government *employees*. We are controlled, and there is zero accountability for their actions.

Consider what occurred in Illinois. People were outraged with those in law enforcement there. Cops have the right to video people at will, but woe to the private citizen who video cops while they are working. It is a felony in Illinois to video cops! A felony! All authority; zero accountability.

It does not take a rocket scientist to determine why they do not want their actions recorded; they are breaking the law themselves. The argument from private citizens is that what cops write in their reports does not parallel reality. They stand behind the government and do as they please, and the rules never apply to them. Unfortunately, this attitude does not apply only to those in law enforcement, which would be bad enough. Regardless of the government entity involved, those who control the rest of us are always exempt from the laws that they enforce.

For example, Congress recently a bill that made it illegal for Congressional members and government employees to profit from insider trading. Huh? The rest of us have lived under these type laws for years! At best, this is very disturbing.

Of course, these are only a few examples of how practical socialism plays out in our daily lives. More importantly, however, these are examples of how to destroy an economy - and a country - but to go a step further, these examples are symptomatic of a larger problem in America.

The Price of Disobedience

Our nation and its leaders abandoned God as early as the 1960s, and perhaps even as early as the 1950s. We have moved from that of a God-fearing nation to a God-less nation in a very brief period, and oh how the mighty have fallen. Most of this occurred in my lifetime, and I am only in the latter years of my 40s. We have removed God from our homes, our schools, our government, and most importantly, our hearts. By my account, we have also removed him from many of our churches.

We masquerade our nation as a Christian nation, but we certainly are not a nation of Christians. God's word depicts the current state of the United States clearly in Isaiah 29:13, " . . . this people draw near with their words and honor me with their lip service, but they remove their hearts far from me, and their reverence for me consists of tradition learned by rote [habit] . . ." (bracketed commentary mine). We have sacrificed the very one with whom our success is held. We have abandoned God. We no longer seek him, and we no longer obey him; and consequently, there is a price to be paid. Welcome to the United States of America, a fallen nation.

Refer back to the text and consider the passing of Joseph's generation in light of the narrative that follows, coupled with the fact that our own nation has perpetually engaged in sin against God. The parallels and subsequent ramifications of such deliberant abandonment are nothing less than astounding - and scary.

The sons of Israel (Joseph's father) greatly multiplied and became exceedingly mighty (see Exodus 1:7). Think about that for a minute while it settles into your mind. The people *greatly* multiplied. Does this not sound oddly analogous to the baby-boom generation of our day? The people multiplied and became mighty; so what? Well, look what happened . . .

> Now a new king arose over Egypt, who did not know Joseph. And he said to his people, "Behold, the people of the sons of Israel are more and mightier than we. Come let us deal wisely with them [Deal wisely? This sounds strikingly synonymous to, let us *control* them.], lest they multiply and in the event of war, they also join themselves to those who hate us [Imagine that; the people in captivity may actually hate the taskmasters!], and fight against us, and depart from the land (Exodus 1:8-10, emphasis mine; bracketed commentary mine).

Amazing! God's people are paying a huge price for the earlier decisions of their ancestors. They no longer have a Godly man like Joseph leading them, and these new leaders no longer seek God - and they no longer obey him. With

Joseph's passing, the Israelites eventually placed their faith fully in a godless government to provide for their needs rather than God, himself. This act represented a significant step toward the demise of God's people. Their earlier decision to sell their possessions to the government in exchange for food sounded as if it was a wise decision - at least while a Godly man was in power. However, this would be a decision they would regret for some 430 long painful years, day after day after day, and generation after generation after generation.

Such is the case in America. We have made poor decisions, decisions laced with sin repeatedly, to the point where we no longer depend on God. We have sold out to the government. Rather, we have sold out to a corrupt government, one that is completely without God. What a hypocrisy for our current president to utter, "May God bless America," at the end of his speeches, especially coming from someone whose fruits continually show evidence contrary to someone who serves Christ.

Here we find God's people faced with a situation eerily analogous to where we now find ourselves: captive by our own government, captive by people hell bent on destroying America. Remember, by the people, *for the government.* "We the People" no longer matters.

What did the government do to control God's people? " . . . they appointed taskmasters over them to afflict them with hard labor (Exodus 1:11). *Taskmasters?* Who are our modern day taskmasters? Law enforcement officers. Cops. Judges. District attorneys. And, like the taskmasters in Egypt, our law enforcement officers are accountable to no one. All authority; zero accountability. Again, "We the People" no longer matter, as we no longer control America.

Consider the corruption we witness from those in law enforcement on a daily basis. Sadly, many of them have taken what should be considered a noble vocation and turned it into one that is loathed by the people. They speed up and down our highways and back roads with no accountability, no accountability to their superiors, and worse, no accountability to those of us who provide their livelihoods - those of us who literally put food on their tables. They drive 80, 90, 100 miles an hour on our interstates. They run red lights and stop signs galore. How often do they get a ticket? They steal drugs from dealers and then profit from drug sales. They barge into people's homes for relatively no reason and plunder what is not theirs to plunder, destroying people's homes and livelihoods in the process. They bully people as if they are invincible and can do no wrong. They gang up and literally beat to death those who work to pay their salaries (Recall that God's people are now working for free on *behalf* of the king and his government; they sold out to the government, and now their every move is controlled by these arrogant, cocky taskmasters!)

The weak always control the strong, lest " . . . they [the Israelite slaves and modern day private citizens] also join themselves to those who hate us [the Israelite slaves and modern day private citizens] and fight against us [taskmasters, cops, and other government employees]." (bracketed commentary mine) They outright commit crimes to get what they want, operating under the protection of the corrupt brotherhood and the corrupt government, accountable to no one.

I even know of a case where a corrupt cop is wreaking havoc in people's lives, all right under the noses of his friends - a judge, the police, sheriff, mayor, and city manager - all of whom refuse to deal with this person. He has repeatedly committed multiple crimes, but they are swept under the rug since he is part of the *brotherhood.* Sadly, this situation is very close to being reflective of the whole. It is no longer a matter of having a rotten apple; it is now a matter of having a rotten tree, or worse, a rotten orchard! In other words, it is becoming increasingly apparent that an ever-increasing number of persons working in law enforcement at large are corrupt and outright criminal.

Power leads to control, control leads to corruption, and corruption leads to destruction - always. "We the People" does not matter, because "We the People" allow these criminal activities.

How many times have you witnessed, or been a part of, situations on the highway when officers issued tickets for speeding, all while doing the same exact thing immediately prior to, and after, stopping others for speeding. On one occasion, I had just moved into the left hand lane to turn left. I was in an expensive sports car that I owned at the time. The car was red with a high performance engine, and it was a convertible. I saw him coming from 3 miles back on a flat stretch of highway, flying in the left hand lane, intimidating all other cars to move out of his way by driving right up behind them - riding their bumper. I was around a half mile to my turn, so I stayed in the left hand lane when he approached me. I was driving 55 mph, exactly. He could not stand it. How dare some rich young person in a car that cost five times his yearly income consider not getting out of his way! How dare that person!

While writing the ticket I asked what the problem was, and noted that I certainly was not speeding. He simply said, "Left lane usage." Left lane usage? This was nothing more than abuse of police power. He was the one who should have received a ticket for left lane usage. The judge felt the same way, surprisingly, and the money I paid my attorney to prove my case in the presence of this crooked cop so I would not have to pay the ticket was worth every penny! The look on the cop's face was priceless!

Many of us have countless stories regarding police intimidation, corruption, and crime. On another occasion, I was stopped for speeding, and I was guilty. I deserved a ticket. Telling however, after discussing the fact that I was guilty, just like all the cops who run up and down our interstates, the cop said, "Well, you know, speeding for state troopers is just a fringe benefit of the job."

I passed one of our fine troopers today. I was going 55 mph on a back road. He was going well over 100 mph with no light on, but do not forget; he was just exercising his fridge benefits. On another occasion, I was stopped for what the officer referred to as "speeding," though he had no radar. I was not speeding at all; rather, I was accelerating rather quickly in a sports car. Cops do not know the difference between speed, velocity, and acceleration,[4] yet they are responsible for enforcing speed limits.

Certainly, we are not worried about something as silly as law enforcement's lack of accountability to those of us

---

[4]   Speed is a scalar quantity, while velocity and acceleration are vector quantities.

who put the food on their table, are we? Of course not. He is a law enforcement officer, a public servant. Unfortunately, most are just cops. He, and many more like him, gives the term public servant a bad name. What a disgrace to those persons in law enforcement who try to do a good job, and do it legally and morally.

So why the fuss over these small issues? Because how cops handle small issues is representative of how they respond when it comes to issues that are more significant. For example, remember Rodney King? Run a search over the internet and you will find images, videos, and articles on hundreds of police beatings! Four Los Angeles cops, those same persons who run up and down our highways with no accountability, nearly beat King to death while more than 10 other cops stood by and watched, as the helpless victim lay lifeless in a pool of his own blood. Were the cops not just as guilty as King after they nearly beat him to death? Certainly.

However, they stand behind their shinny badges issued by the government. All four cops were acquitted of any wrongdoing (surprise, surprise), igniting the LA Riots of 1992. Taskmasters rule! Only later, in another trial, were two of the officers finally convicted. Unfortunately, their convictions required a major public outcry and the destruction of millions of dollars of property for these cops to be seriously investigated!

As a very telling point here, recall what happened when the people rebelled against the officers, when outraged citizens bore arms and took this matter into their own hands. The cops scattered; they fled. When confronted by "We the People," they ran in fear for their lives, exactly as

God's word stated they would do when confronted by "We the People." (see Exodus 1)

We cannot blame the rioters, though much of their rage was taken out on the wrong people. This is what happens when the fox is guarding the henhouse. This is what happens when the ungodly control the Godly, when we abandon God, when we no longer seek him, and when we no longer obey him. It is a price of disobedience.

Consider the case of a man in our local jail that I know personally. He got into an argument with two sheriff deputies that resulted in some form of tussle or fight. Instead of the two deputies wrestling the man to the ground, they shot the man with a TASER - in the head! Not only did they shoot the man in the head, they shot him in the face! They leads of the TASER hit him in the eyes! He is now blind - for life! Maybe the man was initially in the wrong, or maybe the deputies; who knows? But was it really necessary to shoot someone in the face with a TASER rather than the two deputies wrestling this 175 pound man to the ground? Worse, this gentleman, the victim, is now in the local jail, while the deputies go about inflicting damage to other innocent souls. All authority; zero accountability.

Like the cops who nearly beat Rodney King to death, and the local deputies who permanently blinded this gentleman, our federal, state, and local governments have spiraled out of control. "We the People" no longer control the government; rather, the government controls the people -just as it did the Israelites.

Look closely at the prison population in the United States today. We incarcerate more persons per capita than any other country in the world, and we incarcerate more persons in total than any other country in the world. In fact, the US incarcerates more persons in total than the top 35 European countries combined (Spagnoli, 2012).

The fifteen states with the highest incarceration rates per capita, including inmates in all US prisons and jails, in rank order, include 1) Louisiana, 2) Delaware, 3) Alaska, 4) Mississippi, 5) Oklahoma, 6) Texas, 7) Alabama, 8) Arizona, 9) Florida, 10) Connecticut, 11) Georgia, 12) South Carolina, 13) Arkansas, 14) Missouri, and 15) Kentucky. Massachusetts and Maine have the lowest per capita incarceration rates at 49th and 50th, respectively.[5]

Overall, the current prison population per 100,000 citizens in the United States is 730 persons, compared to an average prison population per 100,000 citizens for all other 219 countries of only 171 persons (International Centre for Prison Studies, 2012), a whopping 427 percent difference! *This means we imprison more than four times as many people per capita in the United States than the average of all other nations combined!* Sadly, we have become so desensitized to living in a police state in this county, that we no longer even notice it.

Note how the United States compares to all other countries on a quartile basis, meaning in comparison with all other countries as all countries are divided into four separate groups based on their incarceration averages per 100,000 citizens in each quartile's population:

---

[5] Data were compiled through various 2009 data sources with the Department of Justice and analyzed by the author.

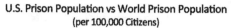

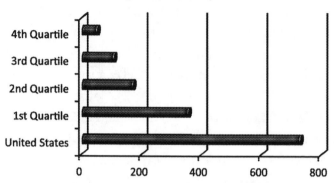

Data Source: (International Centre for Prison Studies, 2012)

Of course, when we begin investigating the facts associated with the heavily skewed prison population in the United States, it becomes quite clear why our prison population rate is a resounding 427 percent higher than the average of all other nations in the world. For example, researchers with the Urban Institute, University of Pennsylvania, and George Mason University conducted an exhaustive meta-analysis regarding the enormous increase in police hiring in the 1990s (Koper, Maguire, & Moore, 1999). The meta-analysis included over 50 prior research studies in the United States regarding the same topic.

The increase in police numbers during the mid to late 1990s explains the drastic increase in local jail populations during the 2000s.

Dr. Koper and his colleagues concluded, "Between 1994 and 1999, federal authorities funded upwards of 60,000 new [police] officers for state and local law enforcement agencies." (p.27) In the end, federal grant money for hiring new officers was so "plentiful" (p.29) that some 100,000 new officers were hired.[6] Federal grant money was the primary reason for this drastic increase in the number of officers hired, *not* a demand from the private sector or an increase in "crime sprees." (p.29) As a point of fact, *crime was irrelevant.* Seventy seven percent (77%) of the increases in the number of new police hires had *nothing* to do with an increase in crime. How telling.

These substantial increases in law enforcement officers are more telling than one would initially think. The decade following this increase resulted in unprecedented increases in local jail populations. For example, the US population increased by 7.2 percent from 2000-2008 (US Population by State: 1790 to 2011, 2011). However, during this same period, the local jail population across the US increased by 26.5 percent (Bureau of Justice Statistics, 2012), a 368 percent difference!

The increase in police numbers during the mid to late 1990s explains the drastic increase in local jail populations during the 2000s. Parenthetically, there are a number of studies to support this claim.

Telling, of the 15 states with the highest per capita incarceration rates noted above, including prison rates and jail population rates, eight of these states also employ the largest per capita number of law enforcement officers. These eight states, along with their national ranking in terms of the per capita number of law enforcement officers each state employs, include Louisiana (1st), New Jersey (2nd), New York (3rd), Illinois 4th), Wyoming (5th), Georgia (9th),

---

[6]   For further study, also see a Bureau of Justice Statistics, US Department of Justice, study by Dr. Brain Reeves: Census of State and Local Law Enforcement Agencies: 2008. July 2011.

Mississippi (11th), and Florida (15th). For example, Louisiana has the highest population of prison and jail inmates per capita, and the state employs the largest number of law enforcement officers per capita. As another example, Mississippi houses the 4th largest population of inmates per capita, while it employs the 11th largest number of law enforcement officers per capita.

Perhaps also telling, of the eight states noted above as having the highest per capita incarceration rates *and* employing the largest per capita number of law enforcement officers, three of these states were rated as "corrupt" during a State Integrity Investigation conducted by the Center for Public Integrity (2012). These three states, along with their respective integrity ratings of their state and local government employees, included New Jersey (35th), Wyoming (48th), and Georgia (50th) (The higher the integrity rating, the more corrupt the state was found to be).

Of these three states, only the state of Georgia actually received an "F" in terms of its employees' level of integrity, meaning that government employees in the state of Georgia are more corrupt than in any other state in the United States. No doubt, at least a portion of Georgia's failing grade can be explained by the fact that more than 650 state government employees in Georgia accepted what amounted to brides in 2007 and 2008 (Center for Public Integrity, 2012). How embarrassing.

Across the United States, a higher than normal level of corruption was brought about by this increase in law enforcement personnel in the 1990s and 2000s. In a Department of Justice study in 2000, researchers determined that a whopping 52 percent of law enforcement officers simply look the other way, or turn a blind eye, to the use of excessive force and police brutality, paying no attention to the crimes committed by their fellow officers, whatsoever. Perhaps even more telling is the fact that 25 percent of the officers concluded that reporting other officers for abuse of police authority was simply not worth their time (National Institute of Justice, 2000).

Consequently, it should come as no surprise that Dr. Ronald Weitzer and Dr. Steven Tuch with George Washington University found the public to have no confidence in local police due to high levels of misconduct and corruption. Seventy eight percent (78%) of whites and 90 percent of blacks stated that cops sometimes stop persons for no valid reason. Thirteen percent (13%) and 34 percent, respectively, of persons stated that they had personally been stopped in the past for no valid reason. Additionally, 57 percent of whites stated that officers use insulting language when talking with people, while 80 percent of blacks felt the same. However, what is perhaps more telling is that the overwhelming majority of people (72 percent of whites and 91 percent of blacks) felt that police use excessive force when making arrests (Weitzer & Tuch, 2004).

To put this study in perspective, the sample size typically necessary for findings of a scientific study to be generalizable across a population is roughly 500 when using one of the various forms of random sampling. The sample size used in this study was a whopping 25,000 persons.

Along with corrupt law enforcement officers, how many judges and district attorneys in this country are corrupt? How many stand behind the so-called "court" every day while simultaneously disgracing the judicial system in the greatest nation that humankind has ever known? How many choose to make our laws rather than interpret our laws? How many families have been torn to pieces by corrupt judges who render lawless, not to mention Godless, opinions with no accountability whatsoever? How many corrupt district attorneys complete illegal acts to support their claims during prosecution? Worse, how many corrupt judges and district attorneys are influenced by corrupt cops?

Apparently, several judges fall into corruption of some form every year. Annually, approximately 100 judges across the US are sanctioned in judicial proceedings (American Justice Society, 2002). In the state of Georgia, my home state, 489 formal complaints against judges were filed with the Judicial Qualifications Commission in 2010, more complaints than ever, but that number was surpassed in 2011, with an astounding 517 complaints being filed. Of the 517 complaints, 37 percent were filed against Superior Court judges, and 27 percent were filed against Magistrate Court judges (Annual Report of the Judicial Qualifications Commission, 2011). The number of complaints the Commission docketed increased a staggering 294 percent from 2010 to 2011. In the past two years alone, 21 Georgia judges have faced disciplinary action (McDonald, 2010).

Even then, however, judges in Georgia are simply "disciplined," "removed," or "retired," with no further action taken, regardless of the level of corruptive or illegal activity. Any so-called serious actions that are taken are conducted in complete secrecy, without those who put them in their positions ever knowing the full extent of their wrongdoing (Judicial Qualifications Commission,

State of Georgia, 2012). Then again, do we really expect fellow judges to take serious legal action against their own friends? All authority; zero accountability.

Of course, this also may explain why researchers of the 2012 study conducted by the Center for Public Integrity ranked the state of Georgia *last* in integrity - and *first* in corruption. Perhaps more telling than receiving an "F," however, is that, on an overall scale of 100, Georgia earned an overall score of 49, the worst score in the nation, clearly establishing Georgia's government employees as the *single most corrupt* in all 50 states. Not surprisingly, over half of all fifty states (26) received a grade of "D" or "F" regarding government employee integrity/corruption (Center for Public Integrity, 2012). Georgia just so happened to be honored as holding first place in corruption!

In years' past, judges were not even required to have a basic education, let alone an understanding of our Constitution. Robert Jackson did not graduate from college, yet he served on the US Supreme Court from 1941-1956. Worse, James Byrnes served on the US Supreme Court from 1941-1942, having never graduated from high school. In their defense, the US Constitution does not mandate that a justice have an education (or law degree), but suffice it to say, it would indeed be helpful (Supreme Court of the United States, 2012).

Sadly, many persons in the judicial and law enforcement community, educated or not, choose to leverage the power we give them to destroy the rest of us. Not all of them, certainly, but *many*. For example, from 2000-2005 alone, over 25 death row inmates were exonerated due to corruption by "officials" (Dieter, 2005). More telling, the state of Texas, the state infamous for executions, has been forced to exonerate 41 persons over the last nine years, Cornelius Dupree being one of them. After being convicted of robbery and a host of other crimes, Dupree was thrown in prison, never to win a single appeal, until officials finally admitted they had wrongfully convicted him - after Mr. Dupree had served a full 30 years in prison and was out on probation (Horton, n.d.).

To date, more than 2,000 persons in the US have been exonerated for crimes they did not commit (MacLaughlin, 2012). William Dillon is also one of these persons. Dillon was convicted in the 1980s of a murder he claimed he did not commit. Only after serving nearly 28 years in prison, losing multiple appeals, and being beaten repeatedly in prison, he was exonerated by DNA evidence proving his claim of innocence. Yet, despite DNA evidence, and the fact that the prosecutor's own eyewitness recanted her story immediately after wrongly accusing Mr. Dillon, the state attorney and police arrogantly refused to acknowledge their wrongdoing (William Dillon Freedom Foundation, 2012); nonetheless, the prosecutor and other law enforcement personnel who maliciously prosecuted Mr. Dillon, continue to live comfortable lives with their families.

James Creamer was sentenced to prison in the 1970s for the murder of two physicians. The prosecution's evidence rested upon testimony of an eyewitness who originally claimed to recall nothing of the event due to being high on drugs. Only after intensive hypnosis sessions set in motion by the prosecutor did the witness recall the events - and allow the prosecutor to imprison Creamer. However, after losing appeals with higher courts, an Atlanta newspaper uncovered tape recordings of the hypnosis sessions made by the prosecutor, where the witness herself claimed to have killed the two physicians, not Mr. Creamer. After being held in prison for two years, Mr. Creamer was finally exonerated. Of course, no ramifications were levied against the prospectors for their actions (Northwestern University School of Law, n.d.).

Until we have laws in this country that serve to criminally punish those who participate in criminal acts such as these, we will have many other Mr. Creamers, many of whom will never be exonerated for the time they served for the crimes they never committed. Corruption is simply out of control in the judicial and law enforcement sectors of government. Those who are power hungry, stand behind the shield of the government - just like Pilate. Remember Pilate? Pilate made the ruthless decision to destroy the one person who was not only innocent, but also *perfect*. While standing behind his authority and blaming his decision on that of others, he sentenced Jesus to death (see Mark 15). All authority; no accountability. The only person who could save his live from eternal damnation, Pilate chose to murder. But, God has a message for these persons:

> Not everyone who says to me, 'Lord, Lord,' will enter the kingdom of heaven; but he who does the will of my father who is in heaven. Many will say to me on that day, 'Lord, Lord, did we not prophesy in your name, and in your name cast out demons, and in your name perform many miracles?' And then I will declare to them, 'I never knew you; depart

from me, you who practice lawlessness.'
(Matthew 7:21-23)

Rest assured, justice *will* be served. God will have no
mercy on the souls of these people. "I never knew you."
Amen! So, for those who have been destroyed by the likes
of these people, fear not, for a day will come when God will
cast these persons into the lake of fire - forever.

In the US, people were addicted to the Casey Anthony
trial, as they were the OJ Simpson trial several years ago.
Anthony was accused of murdering her young daughter
in Orlando. The state presented its case, the defense
presented its case, and the jury rendered its decision: Not
Guilty. She certainly appeared to be guilty, but as one who
watched the trial, the prosecution presented little evidence
demonstrating her guilt.

What is ironic about this case however is the fact that
Anthony was found guilty of lying to investigators during
the search for Anthony's daughter. Investigators themselves
lied on the stand - under oath! Are they not just as guilty of
lying? What is also ironic is the fact that one of the state's
lead expert witnesses completely recanted his testimony
of having found nearly 90 searches for chloroform on the
Anthony computer, and doing so the day before closing
arguments. The expert witness told both the sheriff's
department and the prosecuting attorneys that he had
made a terrible miscalculation.

This evidence was damning to the defense, so much so
that this evidence alone may have been enough for a jury to
convict Anthony for murder. Despite learning the truth, that
the prosecutor's expert had recanted his earlier testimony
regarding chloroform, he went forward in closing arguments

the next day, emphatically lying to the jury regarding the chloroform, while knowing that they were lying.

What happened to the state's attorneys for lying to the jury in a murder case? Did they go to jail? Were they disbarred? Were they even investigated? No. Nothing happened. The lead attorney retired and will draw a state pension the rest of his life, and as for the other attorneys on the prosecution's side, well, they probably received a promotion. Worse, now the lead prosecuting attorney, one of the attorneys who withheld evidence that could have hanged Anthony for murder, has written a book about this trial - and profited from it! How telling.

As if this was not enough, the judge was biased against the defense throughout the entire trial. The poor defense attorney could not utter a word without the prosecution's objections and the judge sustaining nearly every objection - over and over.

A month after the not guilty verdict was rendered by the jury, the judge took it upon himself to place Anthony on probation for writing a bad check, unrelated to the case. He did so without the legal right to do so, without a request from the State, and without notifying the defense. Certainly not all judges operate in this manner, do they? Does working in law enforcement mean you are above the law? Or, does it mean you *are* the law - a *taskmaster!*

The two FBI agents I know do not behave in this manner. They appear to be respectful of the people they serve, and they have always appeared to be very humble. It just occurred to me; both of these men are committed Christians. Hmmm ... This is what happens when the ungodly are in charge. This is what happens when we abandon God, cease to seek him, and cease to obey him. Abandonment and disobedience have infiltrated our very being, placing our entire civilization in jeopardy.

Many government workers, which is *who* the government is, do what they want and dare "We the People" to do anything about it. Business owners have watched this play out for decades. The federal, state, and local governments control nearly every move made by citizens in this country, especially if you are successful.

The weak always control the strong. They do so because the strong are busy earning the American Dream while inadvertently supporting and empowering the weak - and the exponential growth of the weak (not to be confused with the numerical growth of God's people in the text).

The government most often does not typically hire the intellectually perceptive, outside of those in academia. Those persons work in the private sector. As a business owner, I have always sought to hire people very much like me, which is in sharp contrast to what organizational gurus recommend. However, over the years, I have rarely found people like me, and I always wondered why, until a close friend of mine for 30 years and fellow business owner of another engineering firm informed me that he too had gone down the same path, only to finally realize that most people with his work ethic worked for themselves.

Here is a case in point regarding the decision-making ability of many in our government workers . . . My firm is called upon to complete scientifically rigorous and mathematically intensive research studies abroad that involve billions of dollars. Clients base their decisions of whether to pursue these mega projects based solely upon our findings and recommendations. These projects are so important to their nation's economy that presidents and kings of these countries themselves are often involved. Suffice it to say, we cannot afford to be wrong, as our findings affect entire countries or geographic regions of the world. There is no room for error, whatsoever.

In this specific case, the US federal government was involved, and they had to approve the firm completing this particular study. It was the first project with which we had been associated that involved the US federal government to such an extent. The foreign government, the client, was a significant player in Africa, and a country that supplies the world with many, many natural resources. To make a long story short, the foreign government selected our firm to complete the study, and we began discussions with the Ministry of Energy there, though a notice to proceed depended upon the financier of the study, the US federal government. Enter the problem.

After considering our firm for one month, the foreign government selected us to complete the work. After 16 months, the US government finally reached its decision, stating that our firm was unqualified. Ironic; the engineers with the foreign government selected us due to their personal knowledge of our expertise and our previous successful engagements with them, but the attorneys of our own government said we were unqualified - though the person making the decision was not even a US-born citizen. Without boring you with the details of their baseless claim, read my email to them regarding their decision, and draw your own conclusions:

Ms. _____,

Really? Are you indeed saying that we are not qualified to complete this study? Seriously? Ms. _____, this is not our first rodeo. The team of experts we originally submitted has a total of 167 years of experience in the private sector - not as an employee of the US government. Our team of six experts has 167 years of experience planning, engineering, constructing, and operating large international infrastructure projects and facilities similar to the project in _____, Africa.

We have complemented our experiences with 23 academic degrees, including 6 undergraduate degrees, 9 master's degrees, 6 earned research doctorates, and 2 post-doctoral degrees, all in engineering, economics, finance, operations research, and management. Our team holds 7 US patents and has published approximately 700 research studies and written well over 250 reports, papers, and books involving energy generation, transmission, and distribution, as well as energy economics, engineering economics, financial forecasting, systems engineering, and operations research. In addition, our team is licensed to practice professional engineering in approximately 25 countries around the world.

Since our initial team was not qualified to complete this study by your standards, we submitted another team altogether. We collaborated with a firm that has standing contracts with the _____, a firm who has completed numerous engineering projects with the _____, and a firm that has even today an employee in your office working on a similar project. But, as you noted, we are not qualified.

Regards,

Herbert M. Barber, Jr., Ph.D.

26 years of engineering experience

Undergrad in engineering

Two masters degrees in management

Two research doctorates in engineering & economics

Unqualified.

Once a US client felt my firm had overcharged them on a relatively small project. Despite their baseless claim and gross incompetence in the area, the fearless leader for this client took it upon himself to contact the district attorney rather than going through the civil courts. He contacted the district attorney rather than filing a civil claim against us because if he could get the district attorney involved, the suit would cost him nothing. This fearless leader had no access to the financial records of the project or our firm but he just knew they had been overcharged, and far be it for him to be overcharged. Despite having no information whatsoever to support his foolish claim, nor the education, the district attorney moved forward to press criminal charges against us. Yes, I said criminal.

We hired a team of five attorneys, two cost accountants, and a forensic accountant. Our team met with the district attorney, supplying him with all financial data associated with the project. Not surprisingly, the district attorney could not begin to understand the mounds of financial data we provided. He was lost - completely overwhelmed, but he too just knew we had over charged our client. The district attorney was a glorified cop at heart (taskmaster), and cops always think everyone is guilty - everyone but themselves, of course.

He was one of the most ignorant persons with whom I have been involved. His ignorance was irrelevant, however. He *was* the law. He had confused competence with confidence, which is most often the case with those in law enforcement. Or, perhaps his gross incompetence in basic business practices was augmented by his huge ego - and the shield of the government that he stood behind - behind the wall. He could not read financial statements and had not a basic understanding of accepted cost accounting practices, but he did have that wall to stand behind.

Like most government entities, those in law enforcement place a physical wall between you and them. They stand behind physical walls, fences, titles, badges, sunglasses, uniforms, guns, and flashing lights. I never see that in business and industry. Think about it. Those who work in the judicial and law enforcement sector most often refer to themselves as Sergeant Lundy, or Judge Judy, or Captain Hook. How many other vocations or professions do this? Persons in the construction industry do not refer to themselves as Carpenter Joe, or Superintendent Jones, or Engineer Johnson. Neither do persons who work in accounting. "Hey, it's Senior Accountant Adams and Cost Analyst Murphy on the way to meet with Deputy Dawg." Perhaps I should begin introducing myself as Engineer, Economist, Manager, Thinker, and all around Guru, the Grand Pupa, Doctor Barber, PhD, PhD, MS, MS, BS, extraordinaire.

Only after our forensic accountant, one with a Ph.D., 30 years of forensic accounting experience, and the bill rate to go with it, completed a thorough investigation and submitted a large report on our behalf did the district attorney finally yield. By this time, my firm had spent thousands upon thousands of dollars proving what would have been immediately obvious to any business professional with a fundamental understanding of business and the normal protocol associated with cost accounting.

So, what happen to the man (and district attorney) who made false allegations against my firm and me and cost me more money than he or the district attorney would make in years? The same thing that happened to both of them. Nothing. They went about causing grief in the next person's life.

If there were serious criminal ramifications against persons who file false allegations and maliciously prosecute people, "We the People" would never see such unsubstantiated boldness. Since there are no criminal ramifications against these individuals, however, watch how this particular situation played out . . . Because of their attempt to maliciously prosecute my firm, we went to the State Bar Association to request intervention into this district attorney's actions. After talking at length with the director, he concluded that justice should be served. However, we were then informed that the State Bar had no authority over district attorneys, even when it involved a request for disbarment with accommodating evidence in hand. We then talked with the Attorney General in that state; he said that they *did not* prosecute district attorneys. Then we talked with a special prosecutor at the state level, and he told us the same thing. "We do not prosecute district attorneys." We went to local law enforcement in the area as a last resort. Guess what? They too told us the same thing. Finally, we thought, we will go to the federal level, so we contacted the US Attorney General's Office and talked with a special federal prosecutor. Draw your own inferences.

This was nothing more than an abuse of power with malicious intent, and it is exactly what is happening in the text to God's people. The people are being beaten down by the government and more specifically, government employees (The government can do nothing without its employees, so remind yourself of who the government is the next time you discuss the government.).

Those who file false accusations, along with their attorneys, the police who file the false charges, the district attorneys who maliciously prosecute the innocent, and the judges who allow it, should be publically hanged. At a minimum, they should be imprisoned and serve the same prison sentence they were pressing upon the innocent party. There is no room for malicious prosecution in this country, none. Accordingly, God hates:

- a lying tongue
- a lying witness who bears false testimony
- hands that shed innocent blood
- feet that run to evil
- one who stirs up strife
- hearts that plot wicked schemes (see Proverbs 6)

On another occasion a US client of ours chose not to pay our firm a substantial sum of money for services rendered. We completed the work exactly as our contract mandated. What we delivered was well within what would normally be expected for such work, but we even went beyond that, giving them a substantial amount of work at a no charge.

When pressed, the client stated under oath that our services were impeccable. However, the contract was irrelevant to them. Apparently, they never intended to fully pay us. The client's own attorneys told them that they owed the money, but nothing moved them. Fulfilling their contractual obligations meant nothing to them. After numerous depositions and meetings, and forking out over one hundred and fifty thousand dollars in legal fees and accounting fees, we decided to drop the suit altogether. No matter the jury's decision, we had already lost.

We had paid out time and money in legal and accounting fees attempting to force this client to pay, to honor their contract, but hell would freeze over before they would pay. Almost as bad, the judge showed his ignorance in terms of cost accounting in open court. He too did not understand basic business practices and simple accounting practices, ignorantly stating that companies were not allowed to recover overhead costs on projects. We learned quickly that we had been appointed a less than intellectually savvy judge. In the unlikely event that we had won the case, we would never collect what we were owed. It is one thing to win a judgment and quite another to collect. They walked away with a multi-million dollar project of which they only partially paid. We *just walked away.*

We walked away several million dollars in the whole, all due to incompetence and zero accountability. The client benefited from that which he did not work. Apparently in the United States your clients can criminally prosecute you for alleged overbilling with no evidence whatsoever to support their ridiculous claims, but you essentially have no rights when they deliberately and willfully do not pay you for services rendered.

Consider the countless number of governmental agencies in the US. As we do, exactly which Article in the Constitution allows the government to create agencies? Not one Article remotely addresses agencies as an acceptable option for governing the people. For those who do argue a case for constitutional support of agencies, their argument is a bit of a stretch.

Consider OSHA. In 1970, the Occupational Safety and Health Act allowed for the development of what is commonly referred to as OSHA, the Occupational Safety and Health Administration. As an engineer who has spent years working on complex industrial projects, and one who has conducted significant research regarding issues associated with the international engineering and construction industry, I can vouch for the need for some form of support that mandates specific requirements for minimizing or mitigating worker risk. However, based on that same premise, I can also argue that OSHA has taken its mandates too far, so much so that US construction companies are no longer able to produce realistic profits on US projects. Would you take a multi-million/billion dollar risk for a 2 percent profit margin? Not me.

Those who control us are everywhere. Not all, but most government agencies are, in essence, taskmasters. They are there to control the rest of us. While in some cases the initial intent may have been good, the ultimate results are usually not. The more the government controls, the more power they possess, and the more power they possess, the more power they leverage against "We the People." All authority; zero accountability.

Unfortunately, governmental corruption, criminal activity, and evil doing in this country are only getting worse. We have ungodly leaders, and their taskmasters are causing great tribulation in our lives. As was the case with God's people in Egypt, history has proven that the evil attempts of our federal, state, and local governments to control us increase logarithmically with time. For each year that passes, government control increases ten-fold. Consider what happened to God's people in Egypt.

Afraid of the people who provided their well-beings, "the Egyptians [government] compelled the sons of Israel to labor vigorously, and they made their lives bitter . . ." (Exodus 1:13-14; bracketed commentary mine). Who is they? Who made the people's lives bitter? The *government*. The *taskmasters*. And who did we conclude the government is? Its *employees!* Should you need further evidence, read Exodus 3:7:

> And the Lord said, "I have surely seen the affliction of my people who are in Egypt, and have given heed to their cry because of their taskmasters [*because* of their taskmasters, meaning, as a result of, or due to their taskmasters], for I am aware of their sufferings." (bracketed commentary mine)

The taskmasters could not take it; Pharaoh could not take it; the government could not take it. They *feared* the people or, at least, they feared what the people could do to them, which explains the *walls* that our modern day governments use to isolate themselves from "We the People." Is it not telling that a corrupt people, i.e. the government and its taskmasters, would fear a Godly people? Apparently, even the ungodly fear God. Because the taskmasters feared what the people could do to them, they used every means to *control* the people. Such is the situation in our day. In multiple passages, the Bible foretells that these type situations will occur to the Godly.

And indeed, all who desire to live Godly in Christ Jesus will be prosecuted [Not might be prosecuted, but *will be* prosecuted]. But evil men and imposters [those claiming to live Godly lives] will proceed from bad to worse, deceiving and being deceived. (II Timothy 3:12-13, bracketed commentary mine)

. . . lawlessness will be increased [in the latter days] . . . (Matthew 24:12, bracketed commentary mine)

Perhaps more important, however, God's word tells us exactly how he will deal with these situations and the people involved.

For the ruthless will come to an end, and the scorner will be finished. Indeed all who are intent on doing evil will be cut off; who cause a person to be indicted by a word . . . and defraud the one in the right with meaningless arguments. (Isaiah 29:20-21)

"Woe to the rebellious children," declares the Lord, "Who execute a plan, but not mine." (Isaiah 30:1)

How much longer will God tolerate the wickedness in America? How much longer will he tolerate evil? Our day makes the days of Sodom and Gomorrah look like Disney

World, and he destroyed those cities. Consider a few random and seemingly insignificant everyday events in America . . .

- The lead attorney for the Department of Family and Children's Services in my city is a lesbian. Would you not say that using lesbian and family in the same sentence is slightly oxymoronic?
- President Bush appointed a lesbian as one of his close advisors. How can someone reared in the South with a Christian background end up a lesbian? Moreover, why would a Christian ever appoint a lesbian?
- President Obama appointed a lesbian to the US Supreme Court, a lifetime position in the highest court in the country. Surely, her poor values and morals will adversely affect her judicial decisions.
- The people of Massachusetts knowingly elected a homosexual to serve in the US House of Representatives not once, not twice, but 16 consecutive times! Do you really think his liberal views have not influenced his decisions - and the demise of this country?
- A judge recently used the laws of another country to decide a case on American soil. Somehow, it seems this judge should be thrown out of court - and our country.
- The people of the United States elected a man to serve as president who obviously hates America and her Christian heritage. Yet, we leave him in place and call it tolerance and political correctness, all while he continues his rampage of destroying America economically and socially. What is more telling is the fact that people in what proposes to be a Christian nation chose him as our nation's leader.

These are a mere fraction of what we see in this country every day; but to God, it is reflective of an evil, wicked people. To us, it is everyday life in America, but to God it is sin. However, given our fall from grace over the last 50 years, should we really expect anything differently than this? We are none above reproach, and certainly, God somehow loves us all, but how much longer can we realistically expect God to tolerate our sinful ways?

Unfortunately, our fearless leaders are no more spiritually grounded than most in our country. For example, our current president is not the anti-Christ, but he certainly is paving the way for the anti-Christ. Think about it. How else could other countries eventually rise against Israel while the US is a super power and Israel's protector? The United States must first have far less influence on the world at large, and our power is quickly eroding. Our country is bankrupt and our social systems are pathetic. Perhaps worse, Obama is now mandating that the US drastically reduce its nuclear capabilities, all while countries like North Korea and Iran ready their countries to increase their military might. What a huge mistake. In reality, we are the only country standing between Israel and Iran and other demonically controlled countries, such as Russia. Obama has proven the United States will one day too turn her back on Israel, and most likely, sooner rather than later.

But woe to the nation who forsakes Israel.

> . . . I will bless those who bless you [Israel],
> and the one who curses you I will curse.
> (Genesis 12:3, bracketed commentary mine)

Do not overlook the significance of these last few verses. Look back at Isaiah 30:1. Consider those who go about executing a plan other than God's plan. This is where we are in America. Rather than seeking God, obeying him, and working toward completing his plan, we have devised our own plans - which could be better defined as *schemes.*

Have we abandoned God, or has he abandoned us? One thing is certain - we have abandoned him. We have turned our backs on God - and now we will pay the price of abandoning him. We will pay the price of our disobedience. We will pay the price of not following his will, and what a price it will be.

> Behold, the day of the Lord is coming, cruel with fury and burning anger, to make the land a desolation; and he will exterminate its sinners from it. (Isaiah 13:9)

> . . . judgment will be merciless to one who has shown no mercy . . . (James 2:13)

The Egyptian taskmasters ruled with an iron fist, like cops today. What the king said was the law of the day, but what the taskmasters did *ruled* the day. No doubt, they yelled at the people, they intimidated the people, and they beat the people. They controlled every move the people made. The king's people (government employees) literally controlled

All involved were caught in a vicious cycle. The more the taskmasters controlled, the bitterer God's people became; and the bitterer God's people became, the more control the taskmasters levied against them...

the people. And remember who the people here were - the workers, the people who provided the government employees with resources they needed to prosper. The more the government employees prospered, the more they wanted

- just like government employees today. We have become slaves to the taskmasters.

God's people were at a breaking point. Frankly, his people had grown quite tired of it. They had tired of every move they made being controlled by those who did not did not earn their own keep. They had tired of the government prospering at the expense of their efforts. They had tired of working harder and harder and having less and less. The taskmasters knew it, and the government at large knew it. They were heading for serious trouble. It was not a matter of if they were heading for serious trouble; it was a matter of when. It was inevitable. It was only a matter of time before the private sector exploded against the government.

All involved were caught in a vicious cycle. The more the taskmasters controlled, the bitterer God's people became; and the bitterer God's people became, the more control the taskmasters levied against them, lest they rise up against them. The mandates of the rule makers were completely out of hand, just as it is in America now, and the situation was (and is) growing more and more volatile with each passing day.

Why do you think the people in modern day Egypt recently exploded against their government? As if the current uprising in Egypt is not bad enough, the uprising has now spilled over into many countries. For example, the people of Swaziland are now protesting against their government. People are simply tired of being controlled by government employees. Egypt, Swaziland, Greece, England, Zimbabwe, Yemen, Algeria, Bahrain, Tunisia, and other countries - people are tired of being beaten down and they are tired of being enslaved to the government by taskmasters who bleed the livelihoods off the makers of this world.

Look at Zimbabwe. Their unemployment rate is 95 percent (Barber, 2011), yet their leader lives a life a luxury. Professionally, we have witnessed some of these uprisings and had to deal directly with the fallout thereof, so these opinions are not without merit. People are tired of being controlled. Of the few people left who work in America and elsewhere, they have tired of working harder and harder while others, government employees included, steal their harvest. This is the price we pay when we collectively turn our backs on God as a nation - and as a world.

We are close to a very volatile situation in America. As I write these words, the news on television is showing demonstrations across the country. America is a ticking time bomb, ready to explode, with only so many ticks left. God set the standard to which we are accountable. Yet, we long ago decided that we know more than God, despite what God's word says about the useless infinite wisdom of this world (see I Corinthians 3:19). We threw God out with the wash and decided to rule ourselves. Self-rule (see I Corinth. 1:25). We are accountable to ourselves, God's word no longer means anything, God no longer means anything, and the clock ticks. Tic Tock. Tic . . .

The Egyptian government and its taskmasters had serious issues. Our taskmasters have serious issues, and these issues compete among themselves within the individual persons. Take most of those in law enforcement, those who are the modern day quintessential taskmaster. Most have huge egos but little education, and without an education to earn or acquire they have no chance of supporting their egos unless they fill those egos through another means, a means we call *power*. As such, they exchange intellect and hard work for *power*, instant power, and instant gratification - and instant gratification whose cup never fills.

What powerful person in history reminds you of these in law enforcement or similar positions in the US? *Adolf Hitler*. Hitler was unpopular and had few friends. He was lazy and had a poor work ethic, and predictably, he was a horrible student. He performed poorly in in nearly every subject he undertook. However, Hitler had a huge ego and an unsurpassed craving for power. He was a classic sociopath, not unlike the average cop in America. Unfortunately, Hitler could not support his ego through what his personal level of intellect brought so he went after the next best thing - power - just like our own taskmasters. As I have said, unbridled power always leads to control, control leads to corruption, and corruption leads to destruction. *Hmmm* . . . think more broadly a minute . . . think about the US at large relative to this statement.

Consider again the way our justice system operates and the thousands of innocent lives that have been destroyed due to malicious prosecutions. In this country, you are guilty until proven otherwise, and even then, the jury only finds you not guilty, as opposed to finding you innocent. For example, a so-called expert here recently destroyed a family by her false testimony and that of her client. She blindly followed the lead of the sociopathic cop who had hired her to "substantiate" his false allegations. Due to the cop's position, the so-called expert's lack of formal education and experience, and corruption in the judicial system, an innocent family was destroyed -forever. Unfortunately, this is very common in our judicial system, the rule, rather than the exception.

Look at our judicial system further. Consider the infamous polygraph examinations and the countless persons who have been falsely accused by those in law enforcement because they did not "pass" their exam. When persons keenly savvy in measurement (PhDs), e.g. not cops, district attorneys, or judges, review the methods associated with the development of these exams, we shake our heads in amazement at this level of ignorance and gross incompetence. These exams are not allowed in court for a reason. Nonetheless, proponents strive to use these exams on the weary - and woe to the person who succumbs to their corrupt manipulation and influence. You have absolutely nothing to gain from taking a polygraph exam, but everything to lose.

I can confidently and without reservation professionally state that polygraph exams are laced with everything *but* scientific validity. In the scientific community (those who have earned PhDs in statistics, measurement, psychology, education, and engineering from accredited research universities), polygraph testing is a joke. Those who push for the utilization of these exams in court demonstrate their gross incompetence, overwhelming ignorance, and utter stupidity regarding Measurement 101. On its best day, polygraph testing is a pseudoscience, meaning that its proponents present it as a science, while offering no evidence that it is indeed scientific.

When developing instruments to collect and measure variables, such as those associated with development of polygraph exams, researchers must investigate both the validity of the instrument and the reliability of the instrument. The two can be mutually exclusive to the layperson, I suppose, but in the scientific community, you cannot demonstrate validity without reliability.

Validity is the degree to which an instrument measures its intended constructs, and reliability is the degree to which the instrument consistently measures those constructs. In other words, validity addresses whether the instrument actually measures what it purports to measure, while reliability addresses how consistently the instrument measures these same constructs.

To the layperson, you can have reliability without validity. You can consistently measure the wrong constructs. This, however, is fundamentally flawed thinking in that reliability is a component of validity. Thus, the researcher, or in this case, the polygraph guru, must demonstrate both reliability and validity, but as you will see, polygraph gurus offer no evidence that validity exists, and they offer no evidence that reliability exists, making these gurus jokes and the so-called development and execution of their exams a pseudoscience at best - or rather, a joke in the scientific community.

That being said, there are three broad types of validity that we consider in the scientific community, two of which polygraph examiners completely ignore due to incompetence. These three types include:
- criterion-related validity
- content-related validity
- construct-related validity

Let me give you a very basic overview of these types. Through criterion-related validity, researchers offer evidence that validity exists between the operationalization of a specific construct, the actual variable, and the instrument used to measure that construct or variable. In so doing, we are able to estimate what we call predictive validity, concurrent validity, and other forms of validity. In other words, we must determine how well the instrument statistically measures the constructs versus how well previous instruments also measure these same or very similar constructs.

With criterion-related validity, we address how well we operationalized our constructs into measureable variables, which is usually addressed through statistical analysis using varying methods, such as basing our research off previous research. Polygraph gurus do not offer evidence that criterion-related validity exists with their instruments. In fact, they do not operationalize their constructs at all, and in so doing, they completely negate any evidence that their instruments have any validity - at all. In fact, it is doubtful that you will find a polygraph guru who has ever heard of criterion validity, let alone one who truly understands it.

Criterion-related validity is one of the most important forms of validity. It can take years of research by countless researchers to fully operationalize constructs. For example, let's suppose I wanted to measure how smart you are, your intelligence. Well, what is intelligence in the first place? How do I define intelligence? Is it how high or low you score on a math test or English test? Or, is it something much more complex? The methods associated with how I define and measure that construct are imperative. I cannot simply say because you did well on your history test that you are smart, or that you have a high intelligence quotient. Years, decades, and even centuries of research by hundreds of researchers go into the operationalization of a construct as complex as intelligence.

Such is the case when the construct is guilt or innocence. These constructs are overwhelmingly complex, and it would take decades to even fundamentally develop these constructs, aside from determining the validity associated with the technology and other methods associated with this type of testing. In a 1980s study conducted by the US federal government, they eventually had to conclude, "The basic theory of how the polygraph test actually works has been only minimally developed and researched." (US Office of Technology Assessment, 1983). Maybe after a century or two, we will have a basic grasp on how to *scientifically* measure these constructs, but not now.

Look even further into this pseudoscience. They claim that they can determine whether you are truthful based upon factors such as your pulse rate. This violates one of the single most fundamental issues in scientific research, that of causation. I cannot simply say that A causes B in these cases. I cannot say that your heart rate increased *because* you were lying. To do so would make you the laughing stock of the scientific community - enter the polygraph guru and thousands of cops and district attorneys.

We simply cannot conclude statistically that your heart rate increased *because* I asked you this question or that question, meaning that you are guilty or innocent. Again, these constructs are far too complicated for novices like polygraph gurus to handle. It would literally take teams of PhDs decades and decades to operationalize these type constructs and then determine actual causal effects. Therefore, at the end of the day, your guilt or innocence cannot be based in the slightest on the fact that some man with a mustache sat you down, hooked up a few wires to you, and asked you a few questions. Their argument is baseless and without scientific merit.

Evidence that content-related validity exists is normally offered by researchers. It is by far the easiest type of validity to "establish," as it is purely subjective. Content-related validity is not much more than that of face validity. In an effort to address content-related validity, the researcher subjectively answers basic questions such as whether the instrument *appears* to measure its intended constructs. There is no statistical method through which content-related validity is offered. It simply cannot be expressed quantitatively, and this in and of itself is a fundamental problem in the scientific community. Therefore, while important, we view content-related validity as lesser evidence that validity exists than with the more rigorous forms of validity. Unfortunately, content-related evidence is the *only* type of validity offered by polygraph gurus.

The third basic type of validity is construct-related validity. Construct-related validity is the degree to which an instrument measures a specific construct or group of constructs. Of the three basic types of validity, it is the most difficult to obtain. Offering evidence of validity of constructs for any instrument, whether those constructs be for a survey instrument, polygraph exam, or standardized test, is a monumental undertaking. Most often, countless independent studies are required to establish the credibility of a construct when offering construct-related validity. Construct-related validity is perhaps the single most important form of validity when it comes to measuring performance-related constructs, but it is one that polygraph gurus completely ignore.

We cannot stop with offering evidence that validity exists, however. We must also determine the reliability of our instrument. Reliability is an imperative component to validity, and we determine our reliability coefficients using various statistical techniques. We will not go into detail with these, but since we have rambled this far, the most commonly used techniques today for estimating reliability include:

- Split-halve reliability
- Test-retest reliability
- Internal reliability (usually using Cronbach's Alpha)
- Inter-rater reliability
- Alternate forms reliability

Unfortunately, polygraph gurus offer no evidence that reasonable reliability coefficients exist - either. Therefore, they certainly offer no evidence that any variance in their dependent variable is explained by their "models" such that their "findings" can be generalized (in a statistical sense).

Even a cursory look at a "study" completed by the American Polygraph Association offers evidence that these self-proclaimed polygraph gurus are quacks. Note the title to their so-called study: *Meta-Analytic Survey of Criterion Accuracy of Validated Polygraph Techniques Report* (Gougler, 2011). This would be funny if so many lives had not been destroyed by these people. For the record, there is no such word in the scientific literature called "meta-analytic." The authors are attempting to use a word they obviously do not understand. It is called meta-analysis, and it is not a survey at all, as they suggested. A meta-analysis is a technique that researchers use to investigate the findings of former studies completed by other researchers, and in so doing, statistically compare the findings of these various studies.

In addition, there is no such term in the scientific literature as the term "criterion accuracy." No competent researcher would use such a word, as doing so undermines the entire thesis that we merely offer evidence that validity exists rather than demonstrating some form of "accuracy" of its existence. Yet further, note how they used the word "validated" in the title. There is no such thing as a "validated" instrument of any kind - especially that of a polygraph exam. No instrument is validated; evidence that validity exists is merely offered. Any competent measurement expert would easily recognize the errors within even the title of the article, not to mention the so-called findings.

Dig further a minute. The researcher who completed this deeply scientific "meta-analytic survey"' whatever that is, was led by a cop who says he has a bachelor's degree in law enforcement and police safety. Seriously? A bachelor's degree? I have five academic degrees, including two earned PhDs from research universities, and I still struggle with these concepts. His deep knowledge base was complemented during completion of the study by another brilliant scholar, one that does not have a college degree - at all. Yet this person felt confident to serve as the lead researcher on this monumental endeavor. Listen friends, confidence should not be confused with competence.

Nevertheless, let's dig even further. The former president of this group of polygraph gurus (American Polygraph Association) was none other than a person who went around claiming that he had an earned PhD, though he did not. The courts eventually learned of his diploma mill degree, including the US Supreme Court, making polygraph "experts" look even worse.

If you took their exam and failed, you may or may not be guilty. Likewise, if you took their exam and passed, you may or may not be guilty. Polygraph testing is a manipulative ploy used by those in law enforcement to control persons they *want* to find guilty, nothing more and nothing less. Concluding their study regarding polygraph testing, the US Office of Testing finally stated, "No overall measure or single statistic of polygraph validity can be established based on available scientific evidence" (US Office of Technology Assessment, 1983). And, nothing has changed since 1983.

Reflect on the use of grand juries in our country. Grand juries are supposed to be selected at random, but are they? We are never told whether the sampling technique used is simple random, [7] which I seriously doubt, or some other form of sampling, like purposeful sampling, which is most likely the case (given that many in our judicial system are corrupt). Simple random sampling requires each person to have an *equal* chance of being selected from the population, and while most people do not fully understand this technique, simple random sampling is arguably the best technique as it reduces the potential for sampling bias over other forms of sampling.

Purposeful sampling is not a representative subset of a population, and thus, scientifically based inferences *cannot* be drawn. Purposeful sampling is close to being what we call samples of convenience, which, like purposeful sampling, produces biased results when one attempts to

---

[7]   There are several forms of scientific sampling, none of which the judicial system uses intentionally.

make inferences to a population, e.g. how the population at large would have rendered an opinion versus how the grand jury selected rendered an opinion. Given that persons who select candidates for grand jury pools are by no means sampling experts, it is most probable that the sample drawn is scientifically biased before the grand jury hears its first case. How unfortunate.

However, regardless whether the sampling technique is scientifically correct, the grand jury is seated and they begin meeting to determine whether a case should actually go to trial, right? If it were indeed that simple, many cases would never go to trial in the first place. In most states, the district attorney presents its side of the evidence to the grand jury, and the grand jury votes it up or down - nearly always in favor of the prosecution, unless he tells them differently.[8] As the defendant, you have no rights whatsoever to stand in front of the grand jury to offer any defense or alternate view of his version of the facts, let alone the actual facts. Nor does your attorney or any of your witnesses - even eyewitnesses. The prosecutor tells the grand jury what they want them to hear, be it the truth or lies, and the grand jury votes to move forward with the trial. How could they not? After all, they have only heard what the district attorney wants them to hear. District attorneys only prosecute whom they want to prosecute, with or without evidence. Accordingly, they should have a 100 percent victory rate during trial.

In fact, district attorneys do have a near 100 percent victory rate when it comes to manipulating grand juries to

---

[8]   In many states, the district attorney does not have to accept the decisions of a grand jury.

indict. Though data associated with grand juries is difficult to obtain, during 1994-1998, the percentage of cases in which the defendant was not indicted was a negligible 0.06 percent, meaning that for every 10,000 cases brought before a grand jury, 9,994 persons were indicted while only six persons were not indicted.[9]

Contrary to what district attorneys would have you believe, grand juries are empowered to investigate any allegations brought forth - *as they want*. They have no rules or guidelines under which they are to operate, again, contrary to what district attorneys would have you believe. They are to meet in secret, with no influence from the district attorney or judge. They are more powerful than any district attorney or judge will ever be. Grand juries are more powerful than even the US Supreme Court. The problem, however, is that district attorneys and judges have slowly and steadily wormed their way into controlling what is supposed to be "We the People." The ultimate purpose of the grand jury is not to be controlled by those who are part of the problem; the purpose of the grand jury is to protect "We the People" *from* the government! From malicious prosecution! From their lies and deceit!

Unfortunately, most persons serving on grand juries are so intimidated with the mere thought of the judicial system in this country that they readily yield to conniving cops, district attorneys, and judges, where in reality, it is the cops, district attorneys and judges who should be yielding. Contrary to reality, grand juries are to conduct their own investigation regarding accusations or charges

---

9   Data provided by Truth in Justice and analyzed by the author (Truth in Justice, 2012).

against an individual, regardless of who made them, and then and only then are they to render an opinion regarding indictment. Grand juries are not to render opinions without first conducting their own *thorough* investigation (which should require days or weeks of effort, not seconds). However, innocent people are indicted in this country every day by bewildered grand juries who unknowingly believe that those in the judicial and law enforcement sectors are honest upstanding citizens just trying to rid the world of evildoers.

Do not be fooled; these persons are not friends of "We the People." Like all persons who work in law enforcement, they arrest first, and ask questions later. They charge you with crimes, and *then* embellish, manipulate, destroy, hide, and falsify statements, events, acts, people, and objects to match their charges against you. Truth has no place in the judicial and law enforcement sectors of our society. The truth is irrelevant - just ask any person who has been wrongly accused.

The same holds true for justice; it is not found in our judicial system, particularly for those who are falsely accused. As one of my attorneys once told me, "Justice is not found in the courtroom. If you want justice to be served, justice is only found on the street."

As a side note regarding grand juries, in many states if you are a cop, district attorney, judge, mayor, representative, senator, or the like, and in the very unlikely event that you are actually being prosecuted, you have the right to present your side of the argument to the grand jury, but again, only if you are *a taskmaster*. Private citizens are exempt from presenting the facts to a grand jury. "We the People" are exempt. Imagine that. This wreaks of corruption from the beginning.

We see this in every walk of life when it comes to our government, whether federal, state, or local. Take something on a very insignificant scale like sign ordinances. Where we live, you cannot put up any form of a small sign advertising anything along the road or highway. Personally, most persons are fine with that to some extent, as we would soon have a surplus of old signs scattered everywhere. Our government takes it to an extreme, though. If your little girl wanted to make and sell brownies, and advertise by putting up a little homemade sign she made with crayons, she would not be allowed. However, and this is a big however, all government entities here, including the large university and two community colleges here, are exempt from the sign ordinance. And we have little cheap signs up everywhere! Imagine that. The government is exempt from its own mountain of rules, laws, and ordinances - always.

Taskmasters come in multiple forms, but they all stand behind their badges, titles, guns, uniforms, sunglasses, cars, and flashing lights and expect all to bow to the power disposed them. They attempt to intimidate you in every way, such as driving around in large black cars, SUVs, and trucks with large bumpers and opaque windows with tinting that is illegal for the private citizen. They destroy what should be very noble vocations (Notice that the word vocation is used here, not profession).

Most persons in our judicial and law enforcement sectors operate as corrupted authorities of a corrupted government, and as power fills the voids of their egos, their corrupted activities grow because their thirst for satisfaction never fills. Like the King of Egypt, they have wasted what could have been a great opportunity for serving the interests of God's people on their own selfish lusts. Like Hitler, as their craving for unearned power grows, they fear it will be taken from them. As the text says, "Behold, the people of the sons of Israel are more and mightier than we. Come let us deal wisely with them," lest they "fight against us, and depart from the land" (Exodus 1:10). Not surprisingly, after thousands of years, nothing has changed.

However, the people are not what taskmasters actually fear, at least not in their eyes. Remember they have guns, badges, and attitudes. Rather than fearing the people, those in law enforcement are dependent upon the people - in more ways than one. Notice the text said, " . . . and depart from the land." They are indeed afraid the people will rise and fight against them. However, they are more afraid that "We the People" will depart from them. They are afraid the people will leave. Such is the case with our government taskmasters. Should they lose the private sector taxpayers they control, they lose their livelihoods; and without their livelihoods, they lose their power, and without their power, their egos are destroyed. They fight to fill the void of dissatisfaction that simply cannot be filled by power, yet not knowing this, they adamantly fight for job security. They fight to control people. Their power turns to control, their control turns to corruption, and their corruption turns to destruction. Ironically, it is these taskmasters who need controlling, not "We the People." The people are just fine. This is what happens when you remove God from the picture.

The government is not full of horrible people. They are not all bad people - or all corrupt. Not all persons in law enforcement are horrible or corrupt. Do not misunderstand the point, but most governmental entities are out of control - way out of control. Government employees are no longer accountable to the private sector taxpayers - the few that are left. Their interests are self-serving. For many of them, everything they do is in their best interest. Forget the term civil servant. They serve only themselves. They want everything those of us in the private sector have, yet they are willing to take no risk to acquire it.

Now, their salaries and retirements are much stronger than those in the private sector, yet they most often have less education and are risk-averse. If you work in the private sector, you too are entitled, I suppose - entitled to work so this massive blob of people can take what you have slaved away to earn - exactly like the Israelites endured for 430 years. Four hundred and thirty long years of government control.

The people employed by our federal, state, and local governments make rules on top of rules on top of rules, and far be it for the people to whom they should be accountable to buck those rules or even argue against the rules. They can buck those rules if they deem it in their personal best interest, but you my friend are but a lowly private sector taxpayer, and you do not matter. They create laws, they create policies, they create rules, all which limit, and these limitations eventually control. They literally stand behind the glass, behind the wall, behind the bench, behind the badge, behind the title, behind the gun, behind anonymous letters on government letterhead, and control us. They now control us to the extent that the few private sector taxpayers that exist are drowning in this wasteland of rules - exactly like God's people. The private sector taxpayer can barely function given the heavy burdens associated with the ever-increasing rules and regulations.

Consider the situation God's people were facing and what happened to them. To set the stage, Moses has now entered the picture. God spoke to Moses through a burning bush (see Exodus 3), calling him to go to Pharaoh and lead the people out of what has become a 430-year bondage, a politically correct word for *slavery*. After significant hesitation on Moses' part, Moses and his brother Aaron, who God also called (see Exodus 4:27), left to confront Pharaoh.

> And afterward Moses and Aaron came and said to Pharaoh, "Thus says the Lord, the God of Israel, 'Let my people go that they may celebrate a feast to me in the wilderness.'" (Exodus 5:1)

Now, watch what happens when Moses and Aaron, two Godly men, confront the ungodly ruler, i.e. the government. Notice Pharaoh's initial response in verse 2:

> But Pharaoh said, "Who is the Lord that I should obey his voice to let Israel go?" I do not know the Lord, and besides I will not let Israel go.

This is a clear demonstration of disrespect on behalf of Pharaoh. Read how he responds more closely. It is as if he sarcastically laughs and says, "Who is this Lord? I do not know this Lord of whom you speak, and besides, I do not care who is he? Do you not know who I am? I am Pharaoh." This is exactly how we have responded to God as a nation over the last 50 years or so. It is not enough that we no longer respect God. No; we now collectively *disrespect* God. How arrogant, how pompous - how damning.

Recall that the people have called upon God for deliverance *from* their corrupt leaders and taskmasters. They are now in captivity because their ancestors sold themselves into what would eventually amount to slavery so they could eat, literally. Then Joseph died, along with all his generations (see Genesis 50:22 and Exodus 1:6), and with the passing of these generations, they lost their moral compass. They no longer had a Godly leader. They no longer had Godly direction. They no longer sought God, and they no longer obeyed God. Though God's people may have remained relatively faithful, despite being in captivity, their leaders did not (Recall that even Pharaoh recognized God when Joseph was seconded as ruler of Egypt). The Egyptians abandoned God, if they ever actually followed him in the first place, despite the fact that the Egyptians had food to eat right along with the Israelites, all due to God working through the leadership of one Godly man. However, with Joseph's passing, now God's people suffered at the hands of the taskmasters (see Exodus 1:11-14 and Exodus 3:7).

There is good news, nonetheless. God heard the pleas of his people (see Exodus 2:23-24) and took notice of them (see Exodus 2:25 and Exodus 3:7).

These are personally bothersome passages. The Israelites literally sold themselves to the government. They sold themselves into slavery. Perhaps some would argue that it was fine for them to sell out to the government since Joseph had a long history of obeying God, and I can personally understand that point since God ordained Joseph specifically to save his people. Contrary to this argument however, the Israelites would eventually realize with Joseph's passing and the installation of ungodly leaders, the repercussions of their decision. They placed their very existence in the government and an ungodly leader, as opposed to God.

Before we move further into our study, consider what happened earlier in the story to Moses, prior to leading God's people out of captivity. Let us use this as a means of helping us frame our next discussion.

One day while out, Moses saw an Egyptian beating a Hebrew, "one of his brethren" (Exodus 2:11). Refer to the text:

> Now it came about in those days, when Moses had grown up, that he went out to his brethren and looked on their hard labors; and he saw an Egyptian beating a Hebrew, one of his brethren. So he looked this way and that, and when he saw there was no one around, he struck down the Egyptian and hid him in the sand. (Exodus 2:11-12)

No doubt this was not the first time Moses had witnessed such beatings, along with all the other evil ways of the Egyptians and their government, but this time was different. This time he had seen enough. This time Moses determined to do something about it. However, what we must understand here is the reason Moses was upset, why he took matters into his own hands. He "looked on their hard labors" and "saw an Egyptian beating a Hebrew" and decided to act. He was tired of the people being controlled by cruel rulers and their government - by taskmasters. Moreover, what we also must take from this passage is the fact that people in America are not far from doing this same thing - taking matters into their own hands, just as our forefathers did when they left England. As with Moses and our forefathers who fled England for America, we are being left with no other choice than to deal with an out of control government.

Allow this situation with the Egyptians to settle in as we observe how he deals with this current situation in Egypt. God's people are suffering at the hands of the taskmasters, the people have called out to God, and he has heard their cries. So, Moses and Aaron have been sent to the king to request the release of God's people. The king refuses, disrespecting God in the process.

Let us look consider what happens after Pharaoh refuses Moses' request to let the people go.

> So the same day Pharaoh commanded the taskmasters over the people and their foremen, saying, "You are no longer to give the people straw to make brick as previously; let them go and gather straw themselves. But the quota of brick which they were making previously, you shall impose on them; you are not to reduce it any. (Exodus 5:6-8)

Pharaoh not only refuses to yield to Moses' request, one that came directly from God, he commands his taskmasters to no longer provide the straw they were previously providing so the people could meet their daily brick quotas. Under no circumstances were the taskmasters to supply the straw, for in Pharaoh's opinion, the people have become "lazy" (v. 8). Lazy? The people who are doing all the work are lazy? Hmmm . . .

Of course, the timing of modern day events could not be more appropriate here. Obama recently stated on television that the US people have become lazy. There is some merit to Obama's comments as fewer and fewer people are working these days, but as for those few of us left in the private sector who work our fingers to the bones day in and day out, and in so doing improve society, we are far from lazy. We are the backbone of America, not the government.

The taskmasters immediately follow the will of the unruly king, just as every good taskmaster would do, and address the "lazy" people. See Exodus 5:10-11.

> So the taskmasters of the people and their foremen went out and spoke to the people, saying, "Thus says Pharaoh, 'I am not going to give you any straw. You go and get straw for yourselves wherever you can find it; but none of your labor will be reduced.'"

Lest you misunderstand what is happening here, let me explain it in no uncertain terms. *The people have become slaves to the government.* If they ever doubted their position in Egyptian society, doubt no more! They have become slaves, like caged animals.

The people are now being led by the ungodly. Who does this sound like? This is America! This is the United States of America! This is exactly where we stand as a nation. We no longer seek God, and we no longer obey him. We no longer work toward completing his will; and of those who do, our numbers are small, very small. Quite simply, we have abandoned God as a nation, and we have abandoned personal mandates of placing Godly men and women in public positions.

Obama's fruits are less than in keeping with biblical principles. Consider his potential upcoming opponent, say Mitt Romney. Well, Romney is caught up in Mormonism, a satanic cult. So, do you want a Muslim or a Mormon? Well, people, we have abandoned God. The very few believers that are left no longer have a say in this country. We are reaping what we have sown. It is as simple as that.

Life now begins to get ugly. Things are going from bad to worse. The government is mandating that the people produce more and more, all while limiting how they do it. Is our government not doing exactly that? Our government has become huge, with the number of mouths to feed steadily increasing every day within their little agencies and bureaucratic entities, along with all the other takers in society. Work slave, work!

The slaves, the workers, the private tax-paying citizen (which, again, is decreasing in number every day) - we are just lazy! Just plain sorry, I guess! It is always the private taxpayer's fault. Even when representatives of the people go to the government in an attempt to explain the impossibilities of the government's mandates, their pleas are rejected - just as Moses' pleas. Like Moses, our representatives are scorned. Consider the situation in the text, and if you are a private tax-paying citizen, consider the text relative to where you stand in America - particularly if you are a business owner:

> ... Why have you not completed your required amount either yesterday or today in making brick as previously? (Exodus 5:14)

> There is no straw given to your servants, yet they keep saying to us, "Make bricks!" And behold, your servants are being beaten [literally in their case, and figuratively and literally in our case]; but it is the fault of your own people [i.e., government employees and the other takers]. But he said, "You are lazy, very lazy . . . So go now and work; for you shall be given no straw, yet you must deliver the quota of bricks." (Exodus 5:16-18, bracketed commentary mine)

This is almost comical. Pharaoh not only says the workers are lazy; he says they are "very lazy." Does this not sound like the United States? The private sector workers; yes, we are the ones who are lazy, very lazy. Right.

The king and his taskmasters are identical to our own president and his taskmasters (Is it not ironic that Obama's taskmasters are called czars?). What do they want when you have nothing else to give? Just a little more. This is what these type people do. They take, and take, and take, until they destroy society. They become so wrapped up in wanting more and more, and controlling us in the process, that they lose sight of reality. The few workers we have left in America who actually work can only provide so much, and we can provide even less when unrealistic mandates and controls are placed so tightly around us. Yet, they want more. After all, in their eyes, they are entitled to it. They want the private sector taxpayers to support them for 50 or 60 years while most only exercise a half-hearted effort of working the first 20 or 30 years in the first place. As for others, we support them their entire lives!

This reminds me of a conversation I had with a person one day regarding the need for his position. He, of course, was a federal government employee, doing nothing in my opinion but waiting to take his long awaited federal retirement that he so much deserved. Like many government positions, his was useless. I argued that he could not make a dollar on his own if his life depended on it, that he had no idea how his check got into his account every month; it just showed up. If his existence relied on him creating an original thought and convincing others to pay him for that idea, he would starve to death. Of course, he adamantly refused my position and boastfully told me how good he was at his job. I backed him in a corner, I suppose, when I told him to put his money where his mouth was. Quit your job tomorrow, and earn your own living, based upon nothing but your own creativity and ingenuity. Suffice it to say, he cowarded-down. Even when I was willing to place money on the table, he cowarded-down. More telling, even when I offered five times his yearly income that he could not *earn* his current government salary in the private sector over the next 12 months using his own abilities, he cowarded-down. If he could not earn his annual government salary over the next year, he would owe me the equivalent of one year of his government income. However, if he struck out on his own and did indeed earn (profit, not gross) at least his current annual government income, I would owe him five times that amount. Of course, we were never going to really make a deal; besides, I am sure that would somehow be seen as illegal.

What a drain on taxpayers. Again, do not confuse confidence with competence.

Like the Israelites, we sit in America. The entitled want more and more from us, but we have nothing left to give. Yet, we somehow must maintain our current quota of bricks, all while gathering our own straw. This is not rocket science. How do these people expect the workers to maintain our brick quantities when they now place extra undue burdens upon us? They don't know, and they don't care. They have no idea how their check gets in their account. As the federal worker noted above, it just shows up. How it gets there is not their problem. That is your problem.

We cannot supply the entire world with the same quota of bricks while increasing the sheer volume of government employees and their never-ending life-long benefits, coupled with even more stringent governmental controls, i.e. collecting our own straw. Even worse than having to collect our own straw, we now must deal with a USD16 trillion debt - with fewer and fewer private sector workers. It is unrealistic, and it is just not going to happen. Yet we act surprised to find that America has collapsed. This is just the price of disobedience.

Saving America

This leads us to an important topic that cannot be overlooked by those who care about this country. It leads us to a discussion regarding how we correct America's path toward destruction, assuming it is even possible, and save it from destruction. First, we must fully understand the positions of the two types of persons in this country.

America produces two and only two types of people - makers and takers. In this country, you are a maker, or you are a taker. You are not both, and though you may have characteristics of both, you will fall out on one end of the scale or the other. In simplest terms, the two groups are defined by who they are, or moreover, by what they do - make or take. The two are diametrically opposed, and their polarity could not be greater. Makers are at one end of the scale, and takers are at the opposite end of the scale. As if their polarity is not enough, the measure between their positions in infinite; it is without measure.

Makers always come before takers. Without makers, there are no takers, for there is nothing to take. It is analogous to capitalism and socialism. Without capitalism, there is no socialism. Period. It is a mathematical impossibility. At the extreme end of the makers-takers scale, we find the backbone of America, the entrepreneurs. Entrepreneurs are those with God-given vision who have the ability to see the world as it could be. They leverage their gifts to make.

Contrast makers with the takers. On the extreme end of the other end of the scale, takers are those who live wholly at the expense of makers. Takers include persons who chose not to work, live in private taxpayer funded houses, and eat taxpayer-funded food. However, takers also include most sectors of the federal, state, and local governments. While a few government employees, and their respective sectors, do not outright fall into the taker end of the scale, per se, they certainly do not fall into the makers' end of the scale. In most cases, government employees are takers. They take from those who make. That being said, the work associated with a few government employees and their respective entities do produce a means and methods for creating private sector jobs, but this percentage is very low.

Very few governmental entities contribute to the US economy. Consider, for example, the US Trade and Development Agency (USTDA). While all of its funding comes from those who make, the agency takes a portion of its funding to fund technical studies. The studies are usually completed by PhDs with significant expertise in economics, finance, engineering, energy, and other fields on behalf of foreign countries that are implementing various infrastructure endeavors. The catch is that the USTDA mandates the host country use US labor and/or materials to complete a large portion of the construction or implementation of the project, thus creating a return on their investment.

Consider our school systems. School systems are packed with teachers and administrators who are accountable to no one. We know this to be a fact; else, teachers would be fired every day for their shortcomings, while others would be financially rewarded for their successes. However, such is not the case. Like all government employees, there is no measure of accountability remotely comparable to that used in the private sector, and thus, government employees waste trillions. Nonetheless, school systems play a significant role in our economy, for without them we would all be ignorant and never produce any worthwhile endeavor. Subsequently, it is difficult to dichotomously qualify school systems as a maker or taker.

Other governmental entities may not directly qualify as a taker, such as a public university. Universities contribute to the US economy by meeting the educational needs of persons. In turn, a few of these persons then go on to further contribute to the economy. The problem occurs, however, when we pay professors to teach and conduct research and they take advantage of the goodness of makers, those who financially make their jobs possible, by working a mere 15-20 hours a week, teaching only one class - or no classes at all, and conducting research that has no chance of doing anything but further increasing our knowledge of a useless discipline.

Several years ago, when I was completing my research for my dissertation I accepted a position as a college professor. I was assigned the normal teaching load of three courses. The first semester was time-consuming due to my having to prepare for three new courses, but it was nothing like that of working in industry. However, I also taught the same three courses the next semester - and was somewhat bored. Having come straight from industry into academia, there was not nearly enough to keep me busy. I was used to working 60-70 hours a week, not 20-25. Therefore, I approached the director of the program and asked to teach two additional courses, for a total of five. However, I was quickly informed that teaching 2-3 courses per semester was considered normal and that anything beyond that would certainly be seen as my trying to buck the system, perhaps even making other professors look bad. I taught there one academic year and went back into industry. Yes, the academic sector of government does help stimulate the economy, but its contributions could be significantly greater. As such, academics contain a mix or makers and takers.

Other governmental agencies are necessary but need overhauling. Consider my only other stint with the government. Upon graduation with my undergraduate degree in civil engineering, I accepted a position with the state government, working on the same bridge project I had worked on when I was an undergraduate student as a field engineer for the contractor responsible for completing the project. I knew I would never get rich with the state, but I was looking forward to a comfortable life.

So much for that idea. A few weeks into the job, the powers-to-be arrived at the project site to gain insight into their future staffing needs. Retirement was eminent among many of the older engineers, and they wanted to determine how we younger engineers felt about our current positions and whether we intended to stay for a career. When I was approached with these questions, my response was, "Well, if you will give me something to do, I will be glad to consider staying here until retirement. But if you think I am going to spend the next 30 or 40 years of my life riding around in a truck all day, with no responsibility (or accountability) and nothing to do, my stint here will be short - very short."

I told them that they had to give me something to do. I had been employed there a few weeks, but I had done literally nothing; we all just rode around and watched people in the private sector work. It was monotonous. It was boring, and it was a waste of my time. We had so many state employees on the project that the contractor's employees had to step over us just to work.

After my response, the powers-to-be then proceeded to inform me that this was the greatest job in the world and that this was the way they operated. Their work procedures were years in the making. Riding around watching the private sector work, all day long, was what I was hired to do - and nothing else. Realizing I could not stomach wasting my time riding around in a truck all day watching others work, I resigned the next day and went back into industry the following week. A lot of nothing goes a long way.

In general, makers are the job creators in society. Again, at the farthest end of the scale are the entrepreneurs. At a minimum, makers are those who actually contribute to the US economy, not to mention, the world economy. Makers need not necessarily be entrepreneurs, but makers rise early, get to work, and put forth a concerted effort all day long to improve their own economic situation and that of the whole. They think about their jobs when they are not at their jobs, always giving consideration as to how they might streamline their areas of responsibility and improve profitability. Contrary to takers, they actually care about this country, and they make an effort of doing something to improve it every day.

At the other end of the scale, we find those who sit at home all day and mandate that others care for them. Takers consist of the want-to-be unemployed, stay-at-home moms (or dads), and most of those who work for the government. They complain because no one seems to care about them; no one seems to understand their needs. Boo-hoo. They sit on their porches all day. They get stressed when their basket weaving class at the community college runs late, making it an almost certainty that they will never make it to school in time to get Junior's brownies to him for his class party. They stay home all day, choosing to let their spouse be the only family member working, all the while driving on the same roads as those of us who chose to work and pay taxes. They stand around and watch others work and demand equal pay. They enforce laws they are above. They render legally binding decisions with no accountability for their actions. They hang around coffee shops. They get to work late and leave early to make up for it. They count the days until they can retire. They take off every holiday and every vacation day, or they save them and deduct those days from their time to retirement, if they even work in the first place. They complain of some limitation associated with their free health insurance. They pay little to no federal or state employment taxes. They fuss about the size of their Social Security check, the one to which they contributed little. They fuss because the privately funded government does not rush to their aid when they foolishly chose to ride out a Category V hurricane. They protest

Herbert M. Barber, Jr., Ph.D.

because we do not commit more money toward saving the habitat of the yellow-bellied polka-dotted opossum in the Congo at the expense of a building a 10,000 employee manufacturing facility in the US. They get handout after handout from private sector taxpayers. They seize every opportunity to legally steal from those who make. Their continued existence is a derivative of those who make. In short, they take. They steal. They drain the makers dry, and in so doing, they destroy America.

As you see, we have makers, we have takers, and the two are diametrically opposed. While there are many do-gooders who try to circumvent this fundamental fact in America, their efforts are in vain. They argue that all men are created equally. These do-gooders fight for equal rights for the takers, right up until when it is equal, and everyone who wants to eat, must work. Despite the best efforts of the do-gooders to redistribute wealth in this country, they have failed to understand that their desired outcome is an unsustainable possibility. It will not work; no pun intended.

For example, in many towns and cities across this country the makers have left the cities for the suburbs. They have left the entire city limits behind to the takers, the only persons left. You wanted it. Here it is. It is yours. The entire city limits; all the roads, all the buildings, the entire infrastructure, everything. So what happens? The takers eventually leave the city, too, following the makers to the suburbs. They have no other choice. They are too sorry to work, and they certainly do not know how to provide for themselves, so they follow the handouts. They follow the source of their existence. And America is beaten down a little further with each passing day.

Overcoming our current horrific economic demise is possible, but it will require change not seen since the Big Bang. No, it would not require the change Obama has given this nation, but it would require change. Believe it or not, it would require one of the main changes that Obama has stressed his entire presidency. So what is this change? What is this wonderful idea? It requires a *redistribution of wealth*. Overcoming our country's economic collapse requires a blatant redistribution of wealth. But not redistribution as you might think.

America has been oppressed for one too many years, and the only secular way to truly overcome this oppression is to redistribute the wealth back to those who created it, back to those who make, and moreover, back to those who made this country great. There is no other way. The ungodly, corrupt pharaohs and their taskmasters can no longer be allowed to control the people. The people who actually contribute to society must be in control - in total control. No longer can the makers be beaten into submission by the takers. No longer will we be led by the ungodly. No longer will we allow our strong work ethic to go in vain, only to be exploited by the sorry and the corrupt.

Let us make it personal. No longer will I sit idly by while the sorry and corrupt destroy my country. Besides, many of these takers are but one or two generations from being enslaved in countries that have accomplished little to nothing socio-economically speaking, e.g. their homelands. Likewise, many, many of the taskmasters are a mere one or two generations from being in other countries besides the US.

This is the United States of America, people. My family has been in this country since 1654 - over 350 years! Not yours; mine! My family was here 122 long years before the United States even existed! My family made this country into a nation. My family made this country great! Not yours. Mine. If you do not like the way we do things here, go home! I will no longer sit idly by and watch people from other countries come in and destroy mine! And, if I feel this way, I can only imagine how the American Indians feel (though one of my great grandmothers is an American Indian).

It is time for action. If you are offended by my strong opinions, you are free to leave my country. There is a flight with your name on it boarding as we speak. I will call and ask them to hold the plane for you. And take your family with you, too; I cannot afford to feed them either! In this economy, I can barely afford to feed mine!

We have long had issues in our social systems – to the point of becoming a socialized economy. People have argued over solutions in these areas as long as there have been problems, which not surprisingly, is as long as we have had social systems.

Makers, especially those few left who are Christians, and especially those who are Christian entrepreneurs, it is time to stand up - not to be counted, but to *do* the counting! Or, we can continue to watch America be controlled by the sorry, by the corrupt, by the ungodly. Again, this "ain't" rocket science. Society should help those who truly need help, not those who ride the system their entire lives. It really is as simple as that. However, on second thought, maybe it should be rocket science. After all, we had no problem putting a man on the moon.

We have long had issues in our social systems - to the point of becoming a socialized economy. People have argued over solutions in these areas as long as there have been problems, which not surprisingly, is as long as we have had social systems. However, contrary to popular opinion the solution is as straight forward as I stated. It is the answer - the only answer. What was it that Charlie Brown said? "It is always darkest before it turns pitch black." Prepare for darkness, for our socioeconomic issues are not going away in America. As much as I would like to offer a secular solution, nothing utilizing secular ideas as its foundation will work, however. The tree huggers and the do-gooders will always find ways to hang on to that which they feel the lazy are entitled.

Realistically, there is only *one* solution to our problem. Forget about redistributing wealth back to those who made it for now, though this is ultimately what has to occur if we intend to operate under any form of capitalism. *We must return to God.* We must seek him, we must obey him, and we must work toward fulfilling his will for our lives - as individuals and as a nation. God is the only one who can save America, period. Nothing, absolutely nothing, else will work.

America has failed because we have failed as individuals. We have individually negated our relationships with Christ. To overcome this issue, and all the other issues in this country, we must individually and collectively turn back to God, and obey him. The opportunity for America to return to greatness is there. It is within our reach. We merely have to reach out and grasp it. However, we must return to him if we want to seize this opportunity and again be great. As an unknown source once said, "The doors to big opportunity swing on the tiny hinges of obedience." How fitting.

The solution is so simple, but we make it so difficult, so complex. Why would God ever allow the greatest nation on earth to get to this point? Why would he allow Israel to get to this point? Let us return to his word once again to see how God responds to this same question of *why*. Go back to where we left off with Moses and Aaron as they initially pleaded with the king to release the people of God from bondage. Let us pick up with Exodus 5:22 and 23, recalling that Pharaoh has just increased the labor of God's people, now requiring them to produce the same quantity of bricks, only with the much stricter mandate of having to gather their own straw first because Moses and Aaron requested their release.

> Then Moses returned to the Lord and said, "O Lord, why hast thou brought harm to this people? Why did Thou ever send me? Ever since I came to Pharaoh to speak in Thy name, he has done harm to this people; and Thou hast not delivered Thy people at all."

Though I am no preacher, I could preach volumes on this topic. This is and always has been a difficult subject for most Christians. Many can relate. It is analogous to asking, "Why does God allow bad things to happen to good people?" The Bible is full of passages in this regard, but somehow, during the pain we experience, the words often fall so short. They fall short of providing comfort, and they fall short of providing answers.

Over the course of nearly 40 years as a Believer, I have proposed this single question with God perhaps more than any other question. Why, God? You told me to do this. I know you did, and I did it. You see the problem here. You see me struggling. You see me searching. You see me asking. You not only have an answer, but you have the solution. Yet you provide nothing. I sit, I pray, I beg, and nothing. I sit, I pray, I beg, and nothing. I grow more and more frustrated with the situation as each day passes.

I really like the way God's word describes the situation. Notice how Moses responds. This is exactly how I would respond. " . . . Thou hast not delivered Thy people at all." Not only were the people not released, you have only made it worse. Now their workload has nearly doubled.

Herein is one of the most perplexing issues associated with following Christ. The question of why occurs repeatedly. The question seems to linger. It lingers with no real answers, so we seek answers from a variety of sources, including our churches. However, our churches today most often fall short when dealing with this question. Unfortunately, what we see coming from many pulpits in America over the last couple of decades does not help address simple issues, let alone help us deal with complex constructs such as why God allows bad thing to happen to us.

For some reason many preachers today seem to preach watered down feel-good sermons; I suppose these type messages makes most congregates happy. Many sermons are so watered down with secularism and the "look at me" mentality that the likelihood of them having any sustainable meaning is nil to none. "Listen; here are the 10 secrets to success, and if you will just follow what I am about to outline in the next 25 minutes, you too can be successful." Some of these messages sound like an info-commercial. Many of today's sermons are so packed with the "look at me" attitude that it is impossible to get anything from the message but some joke that was told. We hear so little reference to God's word these days that I am afraid we are rearing an entire generation of people with no biblical foundation from which to draw when they too are driven to ponder why. Perhaps it is time these pastors stopped being showboating pulpiteers and started being Bible-thumping preachers again.

> For the time will come when they [the people] will not endure sound doctrine; but wanting to have their ears tickled, they will accumulate for themselves teachers in accordance to their own desires; and will turn away their ears from the truth, and will turn aside to myths. (Timothy 4:3-4, bracketed commentary mine)

From my perspective as a pew sitter for nearly 50 years, the more educated the pastor, the more secular the sermon. In some cases today, I cannot tell whether I am listening to a sermon or listening to a self-help seminar; neither uses the Bible, outside of throwing out a verse or two pulled out of context to support some ill-prepared sermon. Unfortunately, those with strong educations have a tendency to be more self-reliant than those without strong educations, those who most often rely directly on God's leading when presenting the Gospel. It is obvious, and while the presentation is not as glamorous and the speech not nearly as polished, the message is usually deeper and more effective.

Perhaps it is far time we all got serious about reaching people for Christ, not just pastors. Only 73 percent of persons professing to be mainline Protestants, e.g. Baptists, Methodists, believe with certainty that God even exists, compared to 93 percent for Jehovah Witnesses, a well-known cult group. The same study concluded that a mere 41 percent of Jews believe with certainty that God exists (Pew Research Center, 2012). Wow!

Consider what occurs as you listen to your next sermon. By my count, the population of self-proclaimed Christians in the world is around 27.7 percent of the world's population of seven billion.[10] This is after deducting the populations of religions that claim to be Christian but are not, such as Mormons and Jehovah Witnesses. This places the number of unsaved in this world at a whopping 5.1 billion people (72.3%). If the number of people who die in the world every year is approximately 56.9 million people (WorldoMeters, 2011), and 72.3 percent are unsaved, roughly 41 million people (specifically, 40,884,480 persons) go to hell every year. That's 786,240 people a week! Breaking these numbers down further, approximately 78 people in the world go to

---

[10] The author used multiple data sources to estimate the world's Christian population. In all likelihood, the actual percentage of Christians in the world is lower than that noted herein, as this estimate includes persons who self-reported, or proclaimed, to be Christians. Unfortunately, in many so-called Christian countries, such as the United States, persons merely claim to be Christians because they live in a Christian nation, their grandparents took them to church as a small child, or for a host of other reasons. While we do not claim to know the hearts of these persons, we can claim with some degree of accuracy that the percentage of Christians in the world is in fact lower than that estimated.

hell every single minute of every single day of the week - month after month, and year after year. Worse, this rate is increasing as the world's population increases - and even outpacing that growth rate, given the booming non-believing populations of Muslims and others. Therefore, in the average 25-minute sermon, while we are all listening to jokes and watered down secular self-help sermons, approximately 1,950 people enter the gates of hell.

Consider the reality of this. By the end of every sermon you hear, day or night, almost 2,000 people have experienced the flames of hell - and the wrath of God! Two thousand people! In a single sermon! That's two thousand grandfathers, grandmothers, fathers, mothers, sons, daughters, uncles, aunts, cousins, and friends. For the typical church in America that holds three services a week, that means nearly 6,000 human beings begin eternity feeling the intense flames and smelling the rotting flesh of their skeletal bodies while you listen to three short sermons.

> By the end of every sermon you hear, day or night, almost 2,000 people have experienced the flames of hell — and the wrath of God!

They all lived on this earth without ever yielding to God, committing the unpardonable sin, and now they are remorsefully spending every second of every minute of every hour forever in the unimaginable heat, stench, filth, and hopelessness of hell - all because they refused to obey God. Perhaps it is indeed time we returned to some old fashioned Bible-thumping preaching.

But, surely a loving God would not condemn man to spend eternity like that, though - would he? Well, let me pose a question for you to ponder. What if you are wrong?

Let us get back to the issue of why. Why does God allow life to be so difficult? Why does he allow suffering? Why does he allow pain? The answer is very easy. Accepting the answer is another thing altogether. Refer to Exodus 6:7:

> . . . and you shall know that I am the Lord your God, who brought you from under the burdens of the Egyptians.

Here is the *why*. Here is God's answer to the why. So you will know that "I am the Lord your God." Nothing more, nothing less. That is it. If you cannot accept this on face value, read further. Move over to Exodus 7 and recall that Moses and Aaron are again being told to confront Pharaoh, demanding that God's people be released from bondage.

> When Pharaoh will not listen to you, I will lay my hand on Egypt, and bring out my hosts . . . And the Egyptians shall know that I am the Lord. (vs. 4-5)

The scene has now been set for God to wreak havoc on the land, to bring out his hosts - to bring out various plagues. This same scene is played out repeatedly in the text. God tells Moses and Aaron to confront Pharaoh, demanding that God's people be released from bondage. Moses and Aaron confront Pharaoh, and Pharaoh refuses to release the people. Without exception, God reinforces his response to Moses when he questions why. Moses poses the why question to God once and only once only, (see Exodus 5:22-23) and God pounces on the question, ceasing an opportunity to emphatically answer the question of why.

Herbert M. Barber, Jr., Ph.D.

Note how many places God answers this single question of why, either spoken by himself or through Moses (and Aaron) to Pharaoh:

Verse	Event	God's Response (Why)
Exodus 6:7	. . . who brought you out from under the burdens of the Egyptians.	. . . and you shall know that I am your God
Exodus 7:5	. . . and bring out the sons on Israel from their midst.	And the Egyptians shall know that I am the Lord . . .
Exodus 7:17	God turns the water to blood.	By this, you shall know that I am the Lord . . .
Exodus 8:10	God sends a plague of frogs.	. . . that you may know that there is no one like the Lord our God.
Exodus 8:22	God sends a plague of insects.	. . . that you may know that I, the Lord, am in the midst of the land.
Exodus 9:16	Spoken during the plague of boils. No such comments made when the Egyptian's cattle die prior to the plague of boils. However, the Israelites' cattle do not die.	. . . to show you my power, and in order to proclaim my name through all the earth.
Exodus 9:30	God sends hail across the land.	. . . that you may know that the earth is the Lord's.
Exodus 10:2	God sends a plague of locusts. No comments were made after God followed this plague with darkness over the land. However, the Israelites had light in their dwellings.	. . . that you may know that I am the Lord.

Continued on next page.

Verse	Event	God's Response (Why)
Exodus 14:4	Pharaoh gives chase to the Israelites.	. . . and I will be honored through Pharaoh and all his army, and the Egyptians will know that I am the Lord.
Exodus 14:17	God instructs Moses to lift his staff and divide the sea.	. . . and I will be honored . . .
Exodus 14:18	God instructs Moses to lift his staff and divide the sea.	Then the Egyptians will know that I am the Lord.
Exodus 16:6	God provides manna.	At evening, you will know that the Lord has brought you out of the land of Egypt.
Exodus 16:7	God provides manna.	. . . in the morning you will see the glory of the Lord.
Exodus 16:12	God provides quail.	. . . and you shall know that I am the Lord your God.

No book I have read over the years has satisfactorily addressed the question of why God allows adversity in our lives. No sermon has satisfactorily addressed this question. Every book and sermon has fallen short in its explanation. Most often, authors and preachers err on the side of God *allowing* suffering rather than God actually *causing* suffering, but either way, for some reason their explanations have never struck the correct chord with me.

Recently, I heard it argued from a pulpit that God does not cause suffering in our lives - of course not; he simply allows suffering. This is in stark contrast to God's word, however. Refer back to Moses' situation, specifically in Exodus 4:21. Here we find the first of several such conversations, those where God tells Moses to confront Pharaoh but then hastens to add:

> . . . but I will harden his [Pharaoh's] heart so
> that he will not let the people go. (Bracketed
> commentary mine)

This conversation between God and Moses plays out on several occasions in the text. God tells Moses to confront Pharaoh, yet in the same breath tells him that his requests will be denied. He tells Moses that he will not only harden Pharaoh's heart, but he tells him how Pharaoh will respond. God consciously and deliberately *chooses* to harden Pharaoh's heart toward Moses' request to let the people go, and each time God hardens Pharaoh's heart, calamity strikes the Egyptians, most often in a terrible way. Turmoil was wreaked upon the Egyptians. As for God's people, those who were already in bondage, their labor was drastically increased as a result of God hardening Pharaoh's heart. Therefore, the Egyptians and Israelites alike suffered, just differently. As we will later see, freedom itself even comes with turmoil, so much so that the Israelites wanted to return to bondage . . . Freedom never occurs without the Cross. God caused the calamity, the strife, the difficulties, the hardships. God *caused* it. He did not allow it; he *caused* it. He, and he alone, caused it, yet we somehow feel we must explain away God's actions. How God must chuckle with our feeble attempts to explain his actions.

> . . . the foolishness of God is wiser than
> men . . . (1 Corinthians 1:25)

Consider other examples involving suffering in the Bible, the main example of which is Job. Job's situation presents a lesson in humility and faithfulness, and in so doing, it also deals with the topic of whether God causes suffering. In addition, it presents some daunting and disturbing events that make even seasoned Christians squirm.

When we find Job, he is without fault, or as the text states, he is "blameless" (Job 1:1). Blameless he may have been; however, as Job went to present himself before God, Satan tags along with him. Can you imagine that? You are on your way to church and Satan is riding in the passenger seat! On some of our Sunday mornings, I think he may even be driving!

Upon arrival, Satan immediately approaches God and a very disturbing conversation between God and Satan begins, one that has always bothered me. Satan negotiates with God for permission to wreak havoc in Job's life, arguing that he can cause Job to stumble, even to the point of cursing God (see Job 1:6-11). "He will surely curse Thee to Thy face" (verse 11). Wow! Satan certainly appears confident in his abilities, even as he stands before God, himself.

Note closely, however, how this conversation played out. In this first situation, as described in Job 1, God allows Satan to bring suffering into Job's life, but we later see in the next situation (see Job 2) that God appears to just offer Job up to Satan for what will amount to even more suffering. Note what God says in Job 2:3: "And the Lord said to Satan, 'Have you considered my servant Job?'" In this case, Satan does not ask God anything. Quite the contrary. He simply approaches God, answers a question or two, and God offers up Job to Satan in a very matter-of-fact manner.

These conversations are disturbing, and by no means will we attempt to address them. However, these conversations are daunting. God just offers up Job without Satan asking, and though we can accept it, it is indeed bothersome. In one case, God allowed suffering, and in the other God caused suffering.

For those who simply cannot see God characterized as anything beyond grace, consider the father of Jesus, Joseph (not to be confused with Joseph, son of Jacob, whom we have been discussing). Of course, the passages describing the birth of Christ Jesus are found in the Gospels; observe how Mary's pregnancy occurs. Recall that she is not impregnated by Joseph. She is impregnated by the Holy Spirit. Do you not think that Mary's pregnancy did not cause difficulties and hardships in the lives of Joseph and Mary, as well as their families? Most certainly, it did, as is evidenced by their immediate departure from their hometown.

God allows suffering, and God causes suffering. What you do with adversity and suffering is up to you. If you are a Believer, your job is to embrace that adversity, and to allow God to use that suffering for his good - for "we know that God causes all things to work together for good to those who love God, to those who are called according to His purpose" (Romans 8:28).

Think of your world more broadly. What does the 2007 economic collapse mean to you? Why did it occur? Well, we have already addressed this question. It literally occurred because local bankers on Main Street loaned huge sums of money to poor people who had no means of ever servicing the debt. No one twisted banker's arms to loan money, not Sallie Mae, not Freddie Mac, not AIG, no one. Local bankers chose to circumvent sound financial practices, loan money to these people, and sell off the loans as quickly as possible. That was the root cause of the world economic collapse, practically speaking. Now, Fannie Mae and her ugly sisters foreclose on the houses of those who actually could afford their homes prior to the collapse, all while being financially bailed out themselves by tax dollars paid to the federal government by the very persons on which they foreclosed! This is nothing less than legalized stealing, and it clearly demonstrates that the rules that apply to the average citizen never apply to an entity that either is the government, or backed by the government.

Did God cause this collapse, or did he allow it? Did he cause this type of corruption, or did he allow it? These questions are open to much debate, but at a minimum, God has allowed these recent events to unfold. However, as you will see in the end, it really does not matter whether he caused these events, or he allowed them.

Let us understand what happens during adversity. Moreover, let us understand with no ambiguity how God uses adversity, pain, and suffering in our lives. We can sum it up quickly. Look back at Joseph's situation as a teenager in Egypt. Through a series of events that began in a pit, God eventually delivered the Jewish nation. In other words, *through* Joseph's suffering, God's people were saved from starvation. And later, *through* Moses' trials and tribulation, God eventually saved the Jewish nation from bondage.

Now reflect on Joseph and Mary's situation. Through God's actions, Joseph and Mary suffered immensely, but *through* their suffering, this divine intervention, God saved their very souls. Through their suffering, God sends his son, Jesus, to save all who will receive him - from the pits of hell, from eternal damnation (see John 3:16).

Reflect back on the situation in Egypt. With Joseph's passing, the country's reliance on God obviously lessened more and more, and the people, especially the Israelites, suffered, but through their immense suffering, God was glorified. Not the Israelites, not the Egyptians, but God. God was glorified. He both caused and allowed events in Egypt to occur, including great suffering, but through the suffering, his objective was to draw his people back to himself and to demonstrate that he *is* God.

Now, let us also look briefly back at Job. Job's situation is far more complex due to the nature of the exchange between God and Satan regarding Job (see Job 1 and 2), but it yields significant findings. If you remember the story of Job, recall that his wife and friends spent a great deal of time trying to determine why he lost much of his family, his health, and his wealth. Essentially all of what made Job, Job, was gone. In a matter of days, God both allowed and caused situations in Job's life that brought him to his knees.

Job's response was analogous to that of most strong Christians today. During this immense suffering, Job waffles back and forth between acceptance and anger, between hope and despair. In Job 2:10, as the calamity comes on hard, we see Job's response to his wife as that of acceptance - and almost hopeful. "Shall we indeed accept good from God and not accept adversity?" However, a mere four verses later we find Job cursing the day he was born when he talks to his friends (see Job 3:1). Job really lays it all out, as we go further into Job 3. In verse 11, he says, "Why did I not die at birth?" More graphically, he says, " . . . come forth from the womb and expire?" He sums up his suffering to his friends in the last verse of chapter 3 this way:

> I am not at ease, nor am I quite. And I am not
> at rest, but turmoil comes.

A little later Job states that he is merely wasting away (Job 7:16), and in Job 7:20, we find Job really starting to address the question of why by asking, "What have I done to thee?" Who wouldn't question why at this point? Worse, we find Job eventually stating, "According to thy [God's] knowledge I am indeed not guilty. Yet there is no deliverance from thy [God's] hand (Job 10:7, bracketed commentary mine).

Serious adversity, particularly suffering, has a way of bringing out the best in us and the worst in us, and it does so almost simultaneously. We go from plateaus of peace to the pits of pain, all within the matter of seconds. Such was the case with Job. Look at Job 16:6. "If I speak, my pain is not lessened. And if I hold back, what has left me?" He continues . . .

> God hands me over to the ruffians [deceitful persons], and tosses me into the hands of the wicked. I was at ease, but he [God] shattered me, and he grasped me by the neck and shaken me to pieces. He has also set me up as his target. (Job 16:11-12, bracketed commentary mine)

This is not good, not good at all. It bothers me to read this as we address this issue. The suffering is now so bad, and has been so long lasting that Job now sees himself as a target, and considering the text, it certainly seems that the arrow meets the bull's-eye with every shot! God has shattered what Job once knew as life. What was once hope has turned to complete despair. "My spirit is broken." (Job

17:1) And, "Where now is my hope? And who regards my hope?" (Job 17:15).

Job's situation has worsened with each passing day. His family is gone; his wealth is gone. His physical manhood has been diminished to a fragment of what once was, and moreover, now his very spirit - that from which his hope was derived - has been broken and shattered. He now questions whether anyone cares about his hope at all. "Will it go down with me in Sheol [a grave or place of darkness without God]?" (Job 17:16, bracketed commentary mine]

> Know that God has wronged me (Job 19:6).
> He has stripped my honor from me, and
> removed the crown from my head. He breaks
> me down on every side, and I am gone. And
> he has uprooted my hope like a tree. He has
> kindled his anger against me, and considered
> me as his enemy. His troops come together,
> and build up their way against me, and camp
> around my tent (Job 19:9-12).

Ironically, we again see a change in Job's spirit just a few verses later:

> Oh that my words were written! Oh that
> they were inscribed in a book! That with an
> iron stylus and lead! They were engraved in
> rock forever! And as for me, I know that my
> Redeemer lives. (Job 19:23-25, *Praise the
> Lord!*)

Job's position waffles back and forth, as he struggles to accept his situation. But forget about understanding it. Job could not care less whether God caused his suffering or God allowed it. He is lost in the gravity of the burden.

For much of the Book of Job, Job wrestles with his struggles. We ourselves wrestle with Job's struggles. We wrestle with his struggles just as we wrestle with our own struggles. We try our best to understand pain and suffering, difficulty and heartache, but to our dismay, we are left with brokenness and emptiness. In the end, we finally concede, but only after we come face to face with the fact that not only is our situation hopeless, our efforts to understand are hopeless. Finally, in our deepest, darkest moment, God responds, and oh, how he responds. After all the turmoil, after all the loss, after all the suffering, after all the pain, and the heartache, God responds to Job in a manner that can only be described by God himself.

> Where were you when I laid the foundation
> of the earth! (Job 38:4)

Where were YOU! Notice that there is no question mark here, not even in the text. Where were YOU . . . when I, the great I AM, the keeper of your soul, laid the foundation of the earth! Read the entire Book of Job to place this one verse in context. It is amazing!

Personally, this is the single most powerful verse in the Bible. Only after significant personal struggle can one begin to understand the wisdom within this verse. It so much puts me in my place every time I question God - which is often. It so much captures who God is for me. I have taken a huge hit professionally and personally over the last few years. The collapse of the world economy, coupled with my own struggles, has brought me to my knees repeatedly. I have suffered greatly, far more greatly than others will ever know. Yet, all the while life goes on for everyone else. Yes, the economy is horrible, they say. Yes, they have their own personal challenges. However, from where I am standing, it certainly gives the appearance that their struggles are but a drop of water in the ocean when I compare what I know of their struggles with mine. This may be your case, as well.

Occasionally some of my struggles are my own undoing, as is the case with all of us, but most struggles I have endured are not. A significant portion of my suffering has come directly from God. He has both allowed me to suffer, and he has caused me to suffer. He has watched me stumble, and he has ensured that I stumble. He has watched me slip off the cliff, and he has pushed me off the cliff! He has even allowed his own people (Christians) to cause significant hardship in my life, hardships that have cost me millions of dollars and years of frustration. And, he has allowed a few non-Christians to wreak havoc in my life.

Therefore, I often question God, and I question hard. I waffle. I waffle back and forth never knowing what my day will hold. Like Job, I am lost in the gravity of each burden, not to mention the gravity of the collective burdens. Will my day be filled with constant praise for merely being alive, or something else that we take for granted - like recognizing the beauty in the smile of my children, or will my day be filled with more grief, hardship, and fallout from the economy or some other works? Will my day be filled with exuberating gratefulness for merely being a child of

God, or will my day be filled with constant woes? Will my day be one of thankfulness for the oneness suffering brings, or a day spent begging God to eliminate the two sociopaths in my life?

During one particular struggle, I was worn down so low that I told myself out of desperation, "People can do with me what they will, but I am a child of God, and they cannot take that from me." One day more recently as I was yet again struggling with what has now become *my life*, I found myself crying out to God in a desperate, pleading manner, begging to know why I must continue to endure hardships of which only one other person I know can even begin to personally understand, God spoke very boldly, yet very softly, to me. In the mist of my pleas, he simply said, "My grace is sufficient." That is it. My grace is sufficient. Brokenness had now taken on an entirely new meaning.

Let me place this meaning in context. His statement meant to me, quite literally, that his grace is sufficient, that he would do with me as he felt necessary to draw me to himself, to that oneness with Christ. In other words, my salvation through Christ, and that alone, was enough. Nothing more. I was saved through grace - and nothing else, absolutely nothing else, mattered. I offered you eternal life; and you accepted. You did not even deserve that. Yours is not to question why. I was stunned. As Job, I was silenced - and, as Job, I was humbled, very humbled. At the end of the day, I am a child of God, and nothing else matters.

God tells Job in specific terms who he is, and who He is. God is frank and direct. Consider some of the verses in Job 38, and recall that these statements are while Job is experiencing prolonged hardship in his life. He has suffered a long and painful hardship, after another, after another. He has waffled between questioning God and praising God. After what must have been an eternity to Job, God answers through Job's brokenness.

> Then the Lord answered Job out of the whirlwind and said, "Who is this that darkens counsel by words without knowledge? Now gird up your loins like a man, and I will ask you, and you instruct me! Where were you when I laid the foundation of the earth! Tell me, if you have understanding, who sets its measurements if you know? Or who stretched the line on it? On what were its bases sunk? Or who laid the cornerstone? (Job 38:1-6)

> "Of who enclosed the sea with doors, when bursting forth, it went out from the womb; when I made a cloud its garment, and thick darkness its swaddling band, and I placed boundaries on it, and I set a bolt and doors, and I said, 'Thus far you shall com, but no farther; and here your proud waves shall stop?' Have you ever in your life commanded the morning?" (Job 38:8-12)

Have you ever in your life commanded the morning? Wow! This leaves me speechless. God's response to Job is incredible! It is powerful! I love it, but honestly, I am glad it is happening to my friend Job rather than me. Can you imagine how Job must have felt in this dress-down from

God? Lest we forget here, recall that Job had nothing to do with why he was standing before God, per se. He did not ask to be in this position in the first place. Job was a God-fearing man. Remember, Job was "blameless" (Job 1:1). In one case, God offered Job up to Satan, as disturbing as that is. As far as we can tell, Job did not deserve to be placed under Satan's wrath, let alone deserve this dressing-down from God. Of course, this is my opinion, and my opinion does not count here.

God's ways are not for us to judge - or necessarily understand. It is not that we cannot question God; it is that we are not in the position to question God. We are not on the same level with God, but when we are as bold as to question, we find that he uses even our questioning to draw us to him. Thus, we can only conclude that our response is simply to *obey*. We are to substitute our questions with simple obedience. Note one of Job's final responses to God. "I will ask thee, and do thou instruct me" (Job 42:4).

The beauty of the story of Job is that God does not stop with allowing and causing suffering in our lives. He makes anew. He restores us - to himself, and he does so in a way that we never knew him. No, our losses are not always restored; recall that Job lost much of his family, and restoration of these specific persons in Job's life never came.

God's restoration is not so much to the things we previously had; he restores us to himself and, in so doing, with a much keener understanding of who he is, and a much deeper relationship with him than before. As such, do not allow yourself to become confused regarding God's blessing and/or his restoration. His blessing and restoration does not always involve your material possessions, people in your life, or some other specific item you treasured. Many, many times blessing and restoration does not. Through every situation, good or bad, God seeks to draw us to himself - so we *will know that he is God* - so we can enjoy oneness with Christ. Our job is simply to *obey*.

Such is the case with America. Our job is to obey. It begins here, and it ends here. We need not think we have to explain God's actions. Our job personally, and as a nation, is only to obey.

Unfortunately, we no longer obey God in America. We have not obeyed him for decades. We have, in effect, abandoned God. We no longer seek God. We seek a relative truth, despite the fact that his word tells us that "every man's way is right in his own eyes" (Proverbs 21:2). We have abandoned the wisdom of our forefathers and the truths they learned in England (see Proverbs 22:28), and yes, in Egypt. We have abandoned God individually. We have abandoned God collectively. And we have abandoned God as a nation.

So how do we save America? Well, we initially obeyed him, and he blessed us. He blessed us in multiple ways, not just materialistically. We grew stronger as a nation. He led, and we followed. Now we go our own way. We do what feels right and chastise the few left who argue against a political decision or judicial decision that is in direct contrast with God's word. We are accountable to no one. We have spat directly in the face of God and wondered why America has fallen. We have disgraced the very one who breathed life

Consider the difference between Joseph, former leader of Egypt, and Obama, current leader of the United States.

into us as a nation, and we show no remorse. Yet we stand perplexed that God has allowed our nation to crumble. We hire ungodly government workers and place them in positions of great authority, then wonder why government controls our very being. We elect ungodly senators and representatives and wonder why they make immoral decisions. We elect an ungodly president to serve as the leader of the greatest nation ever developed and wonder why he makes decisions that disgrace Christians and Jews alike, not to mention God, himself.

Where do we find these corrupt government workers? Where do we find these corrupt senators and representatives? Where did we find such an ungodly president? They were selected by us - *from us.* They did not mysteriously show up one day and decide to destroy our way of life. " . . . Grapes are not gathered from thorn bushes" (Matthew 7:16). These people were drawn from the rest of us. They were placed in their positions by us! Moreover, they represent who we are as a nation, of what we have become. Yet we now wonder how we got in this position, in a position where we are literally controlled by our own government?

Consider the difference between Joseph, former leader of Egypt, and Obama, current leader of the United States. Joseph obeyed God; Obama does not. "You will know them by their fruits" (Matthew 7:16). Look at Joseph's fruits. Now look at Obama's fruits. Despite the rather dismal circumstances that God allowed in Joseph's life during much his early years, he obeyed God. Obama has shown no interest in God. Joseph was a broken man. Obama is a proud man. The text reveals no circumstance where Joseph ever disobeyed God. Obama's actions have been quite the contrary; he hates Christianity but loves Christian-hating Muslims. Through Joseph's leadership, the Jews and Egyptians survived seven years of famine. Through Obama's leadership, we have been set up for seven years of tribulation (literally, the Tribulation Period). Joseph saved a nation; Obama destroyed a nation.

Move forward some 430 years after Joseph ruled. Moses led the people out of bondage. Obama has led the people into bondage. What stark contrasts in leadership. Joseph and Moses obeyed God, and Obama thinks he is God. And it all hinged on obedience.

God's word is very clear regarding how to rebuild America. It was clear from the beginning, and it is equally as clear now. "But seek first his kingdom and his righteousness; and all these things shall be added unto you" (Matthew 6:33). Our forefathers understood this mandate; we do not. "You shall have no other gods before me" (Exodus 20:3). Again, our forefathers understood this mandate; we do not.

In reality, it is not that we do not understand these mandates set forth by God. We understand them fully; we simply choose not to obey them (see James 4:17). "All these things" were added to America *after* our founding fathers obeyed God. Recall that they came to America to worship God freely, not so their worship - and existence - could be controlled by some corrupt group calling themselves government.

The blessing always comes after obedience, not before. Note where the blessing falls out in what is arguably the most well-known verse in the Bible. "For God so loved the world, that he gave his only begotten son, that whoever believes in him should not perish but have eternal life' (John 3:16). Now, do not confuse this with work, for we know that we are saved by grace through faith (Ephesians 2:8), not through our works, so do not confuse this issue. God gave us his only son, and whoever believes in him, will not perish (spend eternity in hell) but have eternal life. God presents his son to us, we believe, and *then* and only then do we not perish and have eternal life.

Consider what Jesus told the lepers in the Book of Luke. As Jesus is on his way to Jerusalem, he meets ten men who have leprosy. Seeing Jesus, "they cried out, 'Jesus, master, have mercy on us'" (Luke 17:13). "And when he saw them, he said to them, 'Go and show yourselves to the priests.'" "And it came about that as they were going, they were cleansed" (Luke 17:14). The lepers were cleansed *after* they believed and obeyed, not before.

Unfortunately, in our fast-food world of having everything at our disposal, we want the blessing before obedience, and worse, we often want the blessing without obedience. Look what God says about blessing here. "Six days you shall labor and do all your work" (Exodus 20:9), and "on the seventh day you shall rest" (Exodus 34:21). If we keep this in context, here rest is part of the mandate, but it is also the blessing. Rest comes after obedience (working), something most in America have backwards.

In America, most people now want the blessing without working at all. Consider the unemployment rate in the United States; it is roughly 8.5 percent now, or so they say. Couple this with the fact that over half of the tax filers in the US do not pay income taxes - at all. Now, hold these thoughts. There are currently just over 307 million people in the US. Of these, roughly 141 million people work full time (US Department of Labor, 2012), meaning that at best these 141 million people must support themselves, plus the remaining 166 million people. However, if we assume that around half of these people do not pay federal income taxes at all,[11] that leaves us with only 83 million people trying to support 307 million people (exclusive of other taxes).

Therefore, the real unemployment rate is not the noted 8.5 percent the government would have you believe; it is a whopping 71 percent! This 71 percent unemployment rate is a far more realistic interpretation of what is going on in America; and this is what happens when we no longer obey God.

God has something to say to the people who chose not to work: " . . . if anyone will not work, neither let him eat" (1 Thessalonians 3:11), but again, we choose to ignore it. Aside from the children who have no parents or caretakers, the people who have substantial disabilities that completely prohibit them from working, and those people who are unemployed but trying to find work, let these people not eat. If they have no interest in working, let them also have no interest in eating. We think we have to sugarcoat everything, but the Bible is very clear. "The desire of the sluggard puts him to death, for his hands refuse to work" (Proverbs 21:25). So, let these people not eat.

Saving America is straightforward. Correcting our path is straightforward. I could argue a case for implementing a true flat tax - a "fee" for living in this country - or develop a plan for cutting government. Or, I could easily develop a plan for creating more jobs in America; that, along with implementing such a plan, would be very easy for someone

---

[11] The percentage of persons who did not pay taxes in the US in 2009, was 42% (Tax Foundation, 2011).

like me. However, God is not going to bless it until we return to him as a nation, and we will not return to God as a nation until we first individually return to him. We are to seek him first. We are not to seek material possessions, or even success. We are to seek God first, and then and only then will we be blessed again as a nation. Again, let us " . . . seek first his kingdom, and his righteousness, and all these things shall be added to you" (Matthew 6:33).

Let us look back to our friend Joseph a few minutes (see Genesis 37), going back a little earlier in his life. Joseph was the son of Jacob. He was Jacob's favorite son, as is evidenced in the text by Jacob making him a multi-colored tunic, or robe. Many people refer to this robe as the coat of many colors.

How is it possible that making this elaborate robe for Joseph, and not his other children, could bring about anything but resentment of Joseph by his brothers? Sibling rivalry has not changed in all these years, and all of us who have children fully understand the shortcomings associated with favoritism, but despite this, the youngest child is often shown a little more favoritism by parents than the older children, and their specialness is substantiated every time we put them upon their pedestal. Such was the case with Joseph.

However, a little childhood favoritism and subsequent envy is not where Joseph's problems with his brothers end, not by far. Joseph is a bit of a dreamer, quite literally, and over the course of time we will see how Joseph's use of dreams lead to his demise, and how they lead to his rise. Note the text beginning with Genesis 37:5-8.

> Then Joseph had a dream, and when he told
> his brothers, they hated him even more. And
> he said to them, "Please listen to this dream
> which I have had; for behold, we were binding
> sheaves in the field, and lo, my sheaf rose
> up and also stood erect; and behold, your
> sheaves gathered around and bowed down
> to my sheaf." Then his brothers said to him,
> "Are you actually going to reign over us? Or
> are you really going to rule over us?" So they
> hated him even more for his dreams and for
> his words.

As an outside observer, you would think that Joseph
would be a bit more reserved in his decision to share a
dream such as this to people who already resented him, but
for some reason, most likely immaturity, and that pedestal
of his, he felt it necessary. However, as if this dream did not
throw a little more fuel on the fire of jealousy, Joseph then
tells them of his next dream.

> "Lo, I have had still another dream; and
> behold, the sun and the moon and eleven
> stars were bowing down to me." (Genesis
> 37:9)

This time, he not only angers his brothers, he angers
his father as well. Therefore, his father lightly scolds him
for the attitude he exhibits regarding his dream. Little did
Joseph know at the time, but boldly stating his dreams to
his jealous brothers was about to be his downfall.

As the next scene plays out, we find Joseph going to check on the welfare of his brothers who are out pasturing their father's flock. Going at the request of his father, I suppose to Joseph it was simply another day. However, upon seeing Joseph in the distance, his brothers quickly devised a scheme against Joseph. They had tired of the favoritism, and by no means were they about to bow down to him as Joseph boldly noted in his dream. The text notes the brothers' sarcastic hatred toward Joseph. "Here comes this dreamer!" (Genesis 37:19) In the brother's defense, how could they have anything but hostility toward Joseph? Not only are they out in the wilderness enduring the elements while Joseph is enjoying the comfort of home, he prances up wearing his flamboyant robe!

Whether Joseph was rubbing his privileges in a bit is not known, but as the youngest brother, almost certainly he enjoyed the benefits that came with being the baby. Unfortunately, the mere sight of Joseph at this point was enough for his brothers to plot not only to put Joseph in his proper place but also to kill him (see verse 20). Upon Joseph's arrival to his brothers, however, his brothers have decided to throw him in a deep pit as opposed to killing him.

> So it came about, when Joseph reached his brothers, that they stripped Joseph of his tunic, the varicolored tunic that was on him; and they took him and threw him into the pit. Now the pit was empty, without any water in it. (Genesis 37:23-24)

Joseph reaches his brothers; they grab him, tear off his glorious robe, and throw him in the pit. How many times have you been treated this way? Joseph obeyed his father and went to check on the welfare of his brothers. Joseph went out in the wilderness to ensure that his brothers had endured no harm, perhaps from bad weather, dehydration, or a wild animal. Yet he is stripped of his clothing and thrown in the pit! And, as if this is not bad enough, pay particular attention to how the text describes the pit. Not only has Joseph been stripped of his beloved robe and thrown in a pit, he has been thrown in a pit that has no water! Should his scheming brothers choose to leave him there, he surely will thirst to death.

However, Joseph's brothers ultimately opt to sell him as opposed to leaving him in the pit. Therefore, Joseph ends up as what amounts to a slave, eventually making his way to Egypt to a man named Potiphar, the captain of Pharaoh's bodyguard. As Joseph fulfilled the wishes of his master, Potiphar notes that God is with Joseph, as in all Joseph does, he proposers. As such, Joseph finds favor with Potiphar, becoming his personal servant and overseer of all he owned (see Genesis 39).

Later Joseph is imprisoned for being falsely accused of, for lack of a better description, sexual misconduct by Potiphar's wife. Of course, as we know, this could not have been farther from the truth. Nonetheless, Joseph is again unjustly punished; he is thrown in prison for this act that he did not commit. Despite dismal circumstances, Joseph works hard and earns the respect of the chief jailer, quickly assuming responsibilities within the jail. Again, "the Lord was with Joseph" (Genesis 39:21).

Moving along with Joseph's current situation, two of the king's servants who are also imprisoned each have a dream (see Genesis 40). Out of desperation, the chief cupbearer allows Joseph to interpret the dream. Joseph tells the cupbearer that he will be removed from prison and restored to his position of chief cupbearer for Pharaoh. Joseph respectfully requests that the cupbearer remember him when he is restored to his position by telling Pharaoh of how he underhandedly ended up in prison. "Only keep me in mind when it goes well with you, and please do me a kindness by mentioning me to Pharaoh, and get me out of this dungeon" (Genesis 40:14). Joseph then interprets the chief baker's dream, telling him that he will be hanged - and hanged he was.

Yet despite Joseph correctly interpreting both dreams and personally asking the cupbearer to state his case to Pharaoh so he might also be released from being wrongfully imprisoned, the cupbearer completely forgets about Joseph. For two additional years, Joseph would live in the filth of an Egyptian prison.

Ponder that situation. Despite being thrown in a pit, sold into slavery, falsely accused of sexual misconduct, thrown in jail, maintaining a positive attitude, using his gifts for God's glory, and following his father's will (both his earthly father and his heavenly Father) - just as it appears there may be a sliver of hope - Joseph endures two additional years in prison. He does his father's will and God's will, repeatedly, yet he suffers for two additional long years of prison, in the wet filth and decaying stench of an Egyptian dungeon. Think of the inhumane living conditions this must have been - and it all came about after he obeyed his father.

Has a situation similar to this ever happened to you? If you are truly a deeply committed Christian, one who both seeks and obeys God, no doubt it has, though hopefully on a lesser scale. Despite seeking God, despite serving God, despite obeying God, you ended up in your own prison, captive to actions beyond your control. And you suffered. God causes suffering, and God allows suffering, but be comforted, "For I know the plans that I have for you," declares the Lord, "plans for welfare and not for calamity to give you a future and a hope." (Jeremiah 29:11)

I have a very difficult time getting my hands around this, as I have experienced some difficult circumstances over the last decade. My family and I have lived our own hell, all due to the criminal actions of others. Like Joseph's brothers, Potiphar's wife, and the government who held Joseph captive, the people who committed these criminal acts have walked away from prosecution repeatedly. Such hidden acts mysteriously occur when those committing these crimes are corrupt cops who are supported by corrupt judges. But woe to those of deceit and wickedness. God has not forgotten your evil deeds.

These sick people; they live in the shadows of others, operating behind the wall of their infinite authority with no respect for the unobservant, let alone their innocent victims. They secretly operate relentlessly under the guise of a paranoid friendliness using their superficial charm to shamelessly manipulate and destroy the innocent with the power behind their lying tongues and unbalanced minds. The worlds of the innocent helplessly revolve around their sociopathic egocentric world, hoping at best to only react to their actions due to the minds of the innocent never being so confused as to comprehend the enslavement brought upon them by these mentally disturbed people. The innocent are powerless to operate offensively against such wicked obsessions.

What type of person would recklessly destroy the lives of others while publically standing behind the power he has disgraced? Who would blame everyone but themselves for their sick behaviors that give a new definition to the word sociopath? Who would physically duck in and out of shadowy obscurities to impulsively stalk the innocent as leaches under the cover of darkness while cowardly and relentlessly pursuing their supreme visions of controlling their prey; all behind the cover of a badge they did not earn, do not respect, and do not deserve? Who would spew vicious lies from their lips against those far superior than he for a decade so he himself could be pitied even once? What parasitic soul would compulsively release their rage against the innocent while seeking an honor reserved for the righteous?

What kind of person would commit such reckless destruction in the lives of others? A sociopath, and once you deal with the ramifications of being targeted by a sociopath, most other problems in life seem to pale in significance.

Saul was a sociopath. He chased David relentlessly, all due to jealousy, and though David could have killed Saul, he refused to stoop to that level. Hitler was a sociopath, also. He sought to destroy the entire Jewish race. So was Ted Bundy, a sick person who ruthlessly murdered people at Florida State University.

Sociopathy is an incurable mental disorder. Sociopaths have no conscious, and as such, they commit acts that the rest of us would never dream; they can, for they experience no guilt, no remorse. To deal with a sociopath is to deal directly with Satan. The sociopath's victim is helpless against such evil demonic forces. The sociopath clothes his deceitful ways in charm. They are masters of charm, deceit, lies, manipulation, and conning. They are leaches, bums. They have no sense of accountability, not even to their own children. They cannot love, or experience love. They live their lives with no concern for others. Dealing with a sociopath is far worse than words can describe.

Only four percent of the population is sociopathic (Stout, 2005), but the destruction inflicted by any one person with no conscious is worse than that delivered by any one hundred million persons with a conscious. They destroy the innocent - their lives, reputations, careers, families, and children. After nearly a decade of dealing with the fallout from two socipaths, I am convinced that socipaths are Satan's angels.

However, let the innocent not be deceived. "God is not mocked." (Galatians 6:7) He is no fool. " . . . Even if you should suffer for the sake of righteousness, you are blessed . . . Do not fear their intimidation, and do not be troubled," (1Peter 3:14) for their scheming behavior and deceitful activities that are wreaking havoc in the lives of God's innocent have not gone unnoticed, *nor will they go unpunished*. Their . . .

Joseph did not ponder his role in society nor how he himself might be praised.

> . . . wickedness burns like a fire. It consumes briars and thorns. It even sets the thickets of the forest aflame; and they roll upward in a column of smoke. By the fury of the Lord of

hosts, the land is burned up; and the people
are like fuel for the fire. (Isaiah 9:18-19)

So again, can you imagine how Joseph must have felt?
Maybe not, but some of us have an idea.

Finally, after Joseph endures those two additional
years in prison, Pharaoh himself has dreams that need
interpreting. Only then does the chief cupbearer finally
remember Joseph. However, consider how nonchalantly the
cupbearer begins recounting his recollection of Joseph to
Pharaoh. "I would make mention today of . . . ." (Genesis
41:9). What? You "would make mention?" What kind of
lame comment is this? This man interprets your dream,
giving you tremendous joy and hope that indeed comes to
pass, and all you can say two years later is, "Well, now that
you mention it, yea, I do recall some young guy in prison
with me that may be able to help you?" That is sad.

Joseph goes on to interpret Pharaoh's dreams,
describing in detail the seven years of abundance and the
seven years of famine that Egypt would endure, and in so
doing, rising from leader of the dungeon to leader of the
kingdom, all in one swift moment. However, the key here is
not that the cupbearer seemed like a shallow person for not
addressing Joseph's fate with Pharaoh after he was restored
to his position of cupbearer. Note how Joseph responded to
Pharaoh upon being asked to interpret his dream.

It is not in me; God will give Pharaoh a
favorable answer. (Genesis 41:16)

Despite the dismal reality that had become Joseph's life,
Joseph remained steadfast in his relationship with God. In

so doing, note that Joseph's position in life, his vocation so to speak, changed regularly. He was a favored son, spoiled teenager, fashion model, pipe dreamer, pit dweller, faithful servant, falsely accused sex offender, chief prisoner, prison interpreter, enduring prisoner, kingdom interpreter, and Godly ruler, but above all, Joseph was a child of God. Joseph did not waste time asking God what he would have him *do* in life. He did not have that luxury. God established his vocation (For substantiation, refer to Genesis 45:8: "Now, therefore, it was not you who sent me here, but God."). Joseph did not ponder his role in society nor how he himself might be praised. He was a faithful child of God, and through his faithfulness, God established Joseph's path. Through his childhood, enslavement, and captivity, God set Joseph on a course that would save a kingdom - and honor God himself, so they would *know that he was God.* Joseph's only job was to *obey.* Nothing else.

Keeping with this idea, however, review those positions again. Prior to becoming ruler of Egypt, not a single position Joseph held was glamorous. None of us would consider Joseph's prior experience worthy of such a high-ranking position as ruler of Egypt. Joseph was used, and he was abused. He was common dirt. He was forgotten. His father thought he was dead, and his brothers had long ago pushed him from their thoughts. Those who purchased Joseph and sold him into slavery earlier in his life had long ago spent any monies they made from the sale. Potiphar and his lying wife no longer had need of him. For all practical purposes, Joseph was no more. He did not exist, and if he did, he did not matter. However, Joseph did matter to God. God had plans for Joseph, despite his dismal circumstances. In truth, God made plans for Joseph *through* his dismal circumstances, through his brokenness, both during and resulting from.

Joseph obeyed, and God blessed. God did not bless and then Joseph obey. No, quite the contrary, but for some reason we have this backwards in America. Reflect on the gravity of Joseph's life; note the supreme struggles Joseph endured. He remained faithful, despite all. He obeyed, despite all. In so doing, he honored God - and saved a nation.

Consider the struggles our forefathers experienced when founding America. Despite all, they remained faithful to God. They obeyed God, and God blessed them. He blessed America. He blessed America so much that we have become the envy of the world. Every country aspires to have the success America has experienced. Every country; even those that hate us. No nation has ever accomplished more. We have everything at our disposal, all because we obeyed God despite dismal circumstances. Despite multiple wars, despite the Great Depression, despite numerous natural disasters, and countless other events, America remained faithful to the keeper of her soul - until she didn't.

And, oh how the mighty have fallen.

Perhaps you cannot really appreciate the trials and tribulations of Joseph and Moses until you see the results through the eyes of God, or until you too have been broken. It is a stretch for us to completely understand their trials and tribulations, but consider the results of their faithfulness in Exodus 14:31:

> And when Israel saw the great power which the Lord had used against the Egyptians, the people feared the Lord, and they believed in the Lord . . .

God sought to draw people to him. Nothing more. Perhaps it is time we in America stopped discussing our faith and started discussing our God. Moreover, perhaps it is time we stopped discussing obedience and became obedient - for saving America will require just that.

Final Thoughts

God's word is very clear regarding disobedience. Obey him, and we will be blessed. Disobey him, and we will not be blessed. God does not bless unrighteousness. For some 185 years, we obeyed God - until we did not. Sometime around 1960 we became less dependent upon God, right up until we were not dependent on him at all.

Unfortunately, this is where we stand as a nation today. As a result, the United States is now a fallen nation. Worse, we are very close to becoming a *failed* nation. After all, we have failed our forefathers; we have failed our children and our grandchildren. Like it or not, America is not likely to recover from her ill-fated ways. It just will not happen, for the only way for that to occur is for us to allow the Holy Spirit to transform America back to where we once stood as a nation. Unfortunately, we will never allow that to occur. We have far too much pride.

Socialism in America has given way to a rudimentary form of communism that has destroyed our nation. We are now a land of takers, a land of entitlement, and subsequently, a land where the government rules so the entitled takers can thrive at the expense of the few makers left. The American Dream no longer begins and ends by seeking God and obeying him. The American Dream now consists of seeking self-fulfillment - doing what you want, when you want, and how you want - while mandating that others provide for you and your family.

God is no longer preached from our pulpits, yet we wonder why apostasy is increasing among Christians (see 1 Timothy 4:1). How embarrassing for the Christian community.

We obeyed God, and our nation was richly blessed, but with that blessing came self-reliance, and with self-reliance came pride - and pride cometh before the fall (see Proverbs 16:18). We no longer obey God because we no longer need God, and now we will pay the price for disobedience. Prepare to reap our harvest.

America is still home of the brave, but it is no longer land of the free.

Make no mistake about it. God has allowed us to fail. We first failed individually, and we then failed collectively. The only way America can return to greatness is for us to individually repent and collectively repent, and friend, that is not going to happen. We have come too far, and there is no turning back. We have too much pride as a nation to subject ourselves to God. Besides, in the words of Egypt's infamous leader, Pharaoh, "Who is this Lord?" How arrogant. How self-destructive.

America is still home of the brave, but it is no longer land of the free. As I pen these words, Congress is considering allowing our government to put some twenty or thirty thousand drones in the air over our country. The mere fact that we would ever get to a point where someone would consider such a request is very telling as to where we are as a nation.

Like nearly all other moves made by our local, state, and federal governments, the idea of using drones is couched in a positive manner, such as using them to track terrorists on American soil and the like, but in the end, these drones will do nothing less than track American citizens. Mark my word. Very soon, law enforcement (taskmasters) will use these same drones to track everyday Americans. Trust me. It will happen.

Strategies such as these are well documented as it relates to government employees controlling "We the People." Bar coding, RFID, and GPS technologies are already being used throughout the world to track pets, livestock, vehicles, ships, equipment, planes, products - and children. These technologies are great tools when it comes to logistics, but unfortunately, these same technologies will soon control all of us.

These technologies are advanced, readily available, and awaiting implementation into the general population. Over the course of the next few years, government employees *will* mandate that chips be imbedded into our foreheads or hands. Of course, they will soften the blow of implementation by couching it as a means of better managing healthcare, illegal immigration, children, senior adults, or the like. However, in the end, these ill-fated endeavors will ultimately do nothing less than control us.[12]

Trust me. "We the People" are very, very close to being given this mandate. And, people will blindly comply by the

---

[12] For those interested, visit the Department of Engineering at the University of Illinois to review a new technology called Smart Skin, a technology developed by teams of engineers, physicists, and scientists that were led by Dr. John Rogers, an MIT educated physicist and chemist; and Dr. Todd Coleman, an MIT educated electrical engineer.

millions - but woe to those who comply, for the price of compliance will be eternity in hell, literally.

> If anyone worships the beast and his image, and receives a mark on his forehead or upon his hand, he also will drink of the wine of the wrath of God, which is mixed in full strength in the cup of his anger; and he will be tormented with fire and brimstone in the presence of the holy angels and in the presence of the Lamb. And the smoke of their torment goes up forever and ever; and they have no rest day and night . . . (Revelation 14:9-11)

The price of our disobedience can be seen everywhere. It is all around us, and it will only worsen in coming years. Our sin has taken us down the road of no return, a road that ends in hell. Now we have a leader who by all indications is intent on destroying America. The election of Obama is reflective of where we are as a nation. Sadly, during the 2008 election, "42 percent of all born again adults voted for Barack Obama" (Barna Research, 2012), and by most current polls, he will be elected again.

No, Obama is not the anti-Christ, but he is certainly paving the way for the anti-Christ. Is he *the* False Profit as described in Revelation 13? Perhaps; but at a minimum, Obama is indeed a false prophet.

Either way, Obama hates Christianity. Therefore, he hates America. What a disgrace. He supports a philosophy that is nothing less than evil - while we allow him to serve in the most powerful position on earth. He openly professes to be a Christian while blazingly ignoring the Day of Prayer in America and simultaneously supporting ungodly faiths. "Beware of the false prophets, who come to you in sheep's clothing, but inwardly are ravenous wolves." (Matthew 7:15)

However, our primary concern should not be that of Obama or others who spew ungodliness and hate, per se. Our concern should be that of *ourselves*. As Pogo, the infamous cartoon character in the Okefenokee Swamp, stated, "We have met the enemy, and he is us." (Pogo Papers, 2008) Obama and other corrupt officials are merely a derivative of who we have become as a nation. The enemy is us. We disobeyed God. And we are now reaping what we have sown.

In the next few years, we will see more and more upheaval in America and across the globe, much like that happening in the Middle East today, and the taskmasters will beat us back. There will be more and more riots against the government and the taskmasters will beat us back. In the coming years we will almost certainly see Obama, or someone like him, play a significant role in world events, flaunting his conniving schemes as an effort of resolving upheaval and conflict, while continuing to undermine the moral and spiritual fiber of civilization. And Americans will let him.

We will see corruption and wickedness in our federal, state, and local governments worsen as our social and economic structures continue their downward spiral. Government employees will seal our fate through more and more control tactics. Our judicial and law enforcement officials will wreak havoc in the lives of average American citizens, even more so than they do today. "We the People" will fight back, and the taskmasters will beat us back. Like the Israelites, there is no hope for self-rescue. With each passing day, life will worsen in America as we move toward the Tribulation[13] - because God does not bless disobedience. But remember; we are receiving that which we asked. We controlled the harvest. Now, prepare to reap what we have sown.

May God have mercy on the United States of America.

---

[13] As was the case with the Israelites who were also captive by their government, God will rapture only his people, i.e. born-again Christians, and spare them from the Tribulation. Note, that God did not save the Egyptian government from death; the Red Sea engulfed them – a point worth pondering. (See Exodus 14)

Behold, the day of the Lord is coming,
cruel with fury and burning anger, to
make the land a desolation; and he will
exterminate its sinners from it.
Isaiah 13:9

References

US Population by State: 1790 to 2011. (2011). Retrieved 2012, from www.infoplease.com/ipa/A0004986.html

WorldoMeters. (2011). Retrieved November 21, 2011, from http://www.worldometers.info/

Truth in Justice. (2012). Retrieved from http://truthinjustice.org/grandjury.htm

US Department of Labor. (2012). Retrieved January 25, 2012, from Bureau of Labor Statisitics: http://www.bls.gov/news.release/empsit.nr0.htm

William Dillon Freedom Foundation. (2012). Retrieved from http://wdffoundation.org/

American Justice Society. (2002). *A Study of State Judicial Proceedings*. Chicago: American Judicature Society. Retrieved 2012, from http://www.ajs.org/ethics/pdfs/Sanctions.pdf

Annual Report of the Judicial Qualifications Commission. (2011). *Annual Report of the Judicial Qualifications Commission, State of Georgia*. Madison: State of Georgia. Retrieved 2012

Barber, H. (2011). *Swazi Energy: The Feasibility of Implementing a Waste to Energy Facility in the Kingdom of Swaziland*. Mbabane, Swaziland: Xicon Research.

Barna Research. (2012). *Christian support for Obama declines*. Retrieved February 21, 2012, from Barna group: http://www.barna.org/leadership-articles/350-christian-support-for-obama-declines

Bureau of Justice Statistics, U. S. (2012). *Jail Inmates at Mid-Year 2011 Statisitical tables*. Office of Justice Programs, Washington, DC.

Cauchon, D. (2010, September 18). *Federal workers earning douoble their private counterparts*. Retrieved 2012, from USA Today: http://www.usatoday.com/money/economy/income/2010-08-10-1Afedpay10_ST_N.htm

Center for Public Integrity. (2012). *State Integrity Investigation.* Retrieved from http://www.stateintegrity.org/your_state

Dieter, R. (2005). *Blind Justice: Juries Deciding Life and Death witho only Half the Truth.* Washington, DC: Death Penalty Information Center. Retrieved from http://www.deathpenaltyinfo.org/BlindJusticeReport. pdf

Eicheler, A. (2011, August 28). *46 Percent of Americans Exempt From Federal Income Tax in 2011.* Retrieved 2012, from Huffington Post: http://www.huffingtonpost.com/2011/06/28/46-percent-of-americans-e_n_886293.html

Gallup Economy. (2010). *State of the States.* Retrieved 2012, from http:// www.gallup.com/poll/141785/gov-employment-ranges-ohio.aspx

Gougler, M. (2011). *Executive Summary of the Meta-Analytic Survey of Criterion Accuracy of Validated Polygraph Techniques.* Retrieved January 30, 2012, from American Polygraph Association: http://www. polygraph.org/section/validated-polygraph-techniques/executive-summary-meta-analytic-survey-criterion-accuracy-val

Horton, S. (n.d.). *In Texas, 41 Exonerations from DNA Evidence in 9 Years.* Retrieved 2012, from http://harpers.org/archive/2011/01/ hbc-90007895

Internal Revenue Service. (2011). *Average monthly social security benifit for a retired worker.* Retrieved October 22, 2011, from Internal Revenue Service: http://ssa-custhelp.ssa.gov/app/answers/detail/a_id/13/~/ average-monthly-social-security-benefit-for-a-retired-worker

International Centre for Prison Studies. (2012). *Prison Population Rates per 100,000 of the National Population.* Retrieved from http://www.prisonstudies.org/info/worldbrief/wpb_stats. php?area=all&category=wb_poprate

IRS. (2011). *History of the IRS.* Retrieved December 7, 2011, from Internal Revenue Service: http://www.irs.gov/irs/article/0,,id=149200,00. html

Judicial Qualifications Commission, State of Georgia. (2012). *Pulblic Judicial Actions.* Retrieved from Judicial Qualifications Commission: http://www.gajqc.com/disciplinary_actions.cfm

Koper, C., Maguire, E., & Moore, G. (1999). *Hiring and Retention Issues in Police Agencies: Readings on the Determinants of Police Strength, Hiring, and Retention of Oficers, and the Federal COPS Program.* US Department of Justice. Washington, DC: Justice Policy Center, Urban

Institute. Retrieved 2012, from http://www.sas.upenn.edu/jerrylee/ research/cops_hiring_retention.pdf

MacLaughlin, M. (2012). *National Registry Of Exonerations: More Than 2,000 People Freed After Wrongful Convictions.* Retrieved from Hufington Post: http://www.huffingtonpost.com/2012/05/21/ national-registry-of-exonerations_n_1534030.html

McDonald, R. (2010). *What's behind the flurry of judicial resignations in Georgia?* ALM: Law.Com.

National Institute of Justice. (2000). *Police Attitudes Toward Abuse of Authority: Findings from a National Study.* Washington, DC: US Department of Justice. Retrieved from https://www.ncjrs.gov/ pdffiles1/nij/181312.pdf

Northwestern University School of Law. (n.d.). Retrieved 2012, from Northwestern University: http://www.law.northwestern.edu/ wrongfulconvictions/exonerations/gaCreamerSummary.html

Pew Research Center. (2012). *US Religion and Landscape Survey.* Retrieved from http://religions.pewforum.org/portraits

Pogo Papers. (2008). *I Go Pogo.* Retrieved 2012, from http://www.igopogo. com/final_authority.htm

Spagnoli, F. (2012). *Statisitcs on Prison Population Rates.* Retrieved from http://filipspagnoli.wordpress.com/stats-on-human-rights/ statistics-on-freedom/statistics-on-prisoner-population-rates/

Stout, M. (2005). *The Socipath Next Door.* Broadway Books.

Supreme Court of the United States. (2012). Retrieved from http://www. supremecourt.gov/faq.aspx

Tax Foundation. (2011, 18 October). *Federal Individual Income Tax Returns with Zero or Negative Tax Liability, 1950-2009.* Retrieved 2012, from Tax Foundation: http://taxfoundation.org/taxdata/ show/25587.html

Tax Foundation. (2011, 21 October). *Federal Spending Received Per Dollar of Taxes Paid by State, 2005.* Retrieved from Tax Data: http:// www.taxfoundation.org/research/show/266.html

The Lockman Foundation. (1975). *New American Standard Bible.* New York: Collins Publishers.

US Department of Commerce. (2011). *Industry Data.* Retrieved November 2, 2011, from Bureau of Economic Analysis: www.bea.gov

US Office of Technology Assessment. (1983). *Scientific Validity of Polygraph Testing.* US Congress, Washington, DC. Retrieved January

25, 2012, from Scientific Testing of Poloygraph Testing: http://www.
fas.org/sgp/othergov/polygraph/ota/

Weitzer, R., & Tuch, S. (2004). Race and Perceptions of Police Misconduct. *Journal of Social Problems, 51*. Retrieved from http://web.missouri. edu/~jlfm89/Race%20Perceptions%20of%20Police%20Misconduct. pdf

Dr. Herbert M. Barber, Jr. has worked in the international engineering and construction industry for over twenty five years. His area of expertise lies at the intersection of engineering economics and decision modeling.

He consults with clients regarding the financial feasibility and economic impact of implementing large industrial and infrastructure projects around the world. Dr. Barber holds five academic degrees in engineering and economics from Georgia Southern University, Florida State University, and Mississippi State University.

He is a son, husband, and father, but most of all, a child of God.